Undergraduate Topics in Computer Science

Undergraduate Topics in Computer Science (UTiCS) delivers high-quality instructional content for undergraduates studying in all areas of computing and information science. From core foundational and theoretical material to final-year topics and applications, UTiCS books take a fresh, concise, and modern approach and are ideal for self-study or for a one- or two-semester course. The texts are all authored by established experts in their fields, reviewed by an international advisory board, and contain numerous examples and problems. Many include fully worked solutions.

More information about this series at http://www.springer.com/series/7592

Martina Seidl • Marion Scholz
Christian Huemer • Gerti Kappel

UML @ Classroom

An Introduction to Object-Oriented Modeling

 Springer

Martina Seidl
Johannes Kepler University Linz
Linz, Austria

Marion Scholz
Vienna University of Technology
Vienna, Austria

Christian Huemer
Vienna University of Technology
Vienna, Austria

Gerti Kappel
Vienna University of Technology
Vienna, Austria

Tanslator
Tracey Duffy
TSD Translations

Series Editor
Ian Mackie

Copyright © 2012 by dpunkt.verlag GmbH, Heidelberg, Germany.
Title of the German original: UML @ Classroom
ISBN 978-3-89864-776-2
Translation Copyright © 2014 by Springer International Publishing AG.
All rights reserved.

ISSN 1863-7310   ISSN 2197-1781   (electronic)
Undergraduate Topics in Computer Science
ISBN 978-3-319-12741-5   ISBN 978-3-319-12742-2   (eBook)
DOI 10.1007/978-3-319-12742-2

Library of Congress Control Number: 2015930192

Springer Cham Heidelberg New York Dordrecht London
© Springer International Publishing Switzerland 2015

Printed on acid-free paper

Springer International Publishing AG Switzerland is part of Springer Science+Business Media (www.springer.com)

Preface

The challenges in today's software development are diverse and go far beyond implementation tasks. They range from requirement specification over system design and implementation to maintenance and further adaptation of the software—to name just a few phases in the software life cycle. In all of these phases of the software development process, many people with different backgrounds and experiences are usually involved. These people need a common language for efficient communication. Obviously, such a language should be as precise as possible without the ambiguities of a natural language. For this purpose, modeling languages have emerged. They are used to create sketches and blueprints for software systems, which in turn serve as a basis for the implementation or even automatic generation of executable code. In the area of object-oriented software development, the Unified Modeling Language (UML) was able to prevail. Of course, to use the language correctly and efficiently, it is necessary to understand the concepts offered by UML. Since 2006, we have offered the course "Object-Oriented Modeling" at the Vienna University of Technology. This course is mandatory for computer science and business informatics students in their first year. Overall, we have up to 1,000 students per year who attend our course. To deal with such a huge number of students while keeping high quality standards, much effort has been spent on the preparation of such a course. This includes the overall organization, course material, and e-learning support. Parts of the course design have been presented at the Educators' Symposium of the MODELS conference [8, 9, 10, 11, 7, 46]. We teach the basics of object-oriented modeling by means of UML.

In particular, we teach

- class and object diagrams,
- sequence diagrams,
- state machine diagrams,
- activity diagrams, and
- use case diagrams

as well as their interrelations. For this purpose, we introduce the syntax (the notation of the language elements), the semantics (the meaning of the language elements), and the pragmatics (how to use the language elements) of these UML diagrams. They cover the most essential concepts of object-oriented modeling and are used in many different stages of the software development process. The course is designed for students who already know the basic concepts of object-oriented programming languages such as Java or C#, but still have no practical experience in software engineering. Based on our comprehensive experience in teaching UML, we wrote the book UML@Classroom. In this book, we address both readers who wish to learn UML in a compact but nevertheless precise manner and teachers whom we want to provide with inspiration for their own course exercises with our extensive example repertoire. We teach UML as close to the standard as possible and illustrate all concepts using intuitive examples. The book is complemented by a website, which contains a complete set of slides to teach the contents of the book as well as teaching videos and e-learning material (http://www.uml.ac.at/).

Software modeling is a very young field of computer science. It experienced an incredible growth within the last two decades. Today, the usage of models goes far beyond pure documentation. Techniques from the area of modeling continually replace conventional programming. Models are far more than just pictures, and modeling is far more than just drawing. With our book UML@Classroom, we want to provide a solid foundation and deep understanding of the most important object-oriented modeling concepts. We aim for rising interest and enthusiasm for this exciting and extremely important field of computer science. UML@Classroom is a textbook, which explicitly addresses beginners and people with little or no modeling experience. It introduces basic concepts in a very precise manner, while abstaining from the interpretation of rare special cases. UML@Classroom is kept very compact in order to allow the reader to focus on the most commonly used concepts of UML. Much emphasis is spent on illustrative examples breathing life into the theory we present.

Acknowledgments

We would like to thank the many people who supported us in the successful completion of this book. Very special thanks go to our families who showed great patience for this book project. We are deeply indebted to Katja Hildebrandt (Vienna University of Technology) for drawing all the figures of this book and for supporting us with a million of other things. We would like to thank Ralf Gerstner from Springer and Christa Preisendanz from dpunkt.verlag for making this English version possible. Further, we would like to thank Tracey Duffy for the good collaboration on the translation of the German version of this book into English and Jeremy Gibbons (University of Oxford) for the careful proofreading and the very valuable feedback. Finally, we would like to acknowledge the input we got from our students over the years which was one of the main motivators for writing this book.

Linz and Vienna, September 2014

Martina Seidl
Marion Scholz
Christian Huemer
Gerti Kappel

Contents

Chapter 1
Introduction

The *Unified Modeling Language* (UML) is a consolidation of the best practices that have been established over the years in the use of modeling languages. UML enables us to present the widely varying aspects of a software system (e.g., requirements, data structures, data flows, and information flows) within a single framework using object-oriented concepts. Before we venture too deeply into UML, however, in this chapter we first explain why modeling is an indispensable part of software development. To do this, we look at what models are and what we need them for. We briefly recapitulate the basic concepts of object orientation before continuing with an overview of the structure of the book.

Unified Modeling Language (UML)

1.1 Motivation

Imagine that you want to develop a software system that a customer has ordered from you. One of the first challenges you are confronted with is clarifying what the customer actually wants and whether you have understood the customer's exact requirements for the prospective system. This first step is already critical for the success or failure of your project. The question is, how do you communicate with your customer? Natural language is not necessarily a good choice as it is imprecise and ambiguous. Misunderstandings can easily arise and there is a very great risk that people with different backgrounds (e.g., a computer scientist and a business manager) will talk at cross-purposes, which can have serious consequences.

What you need is to be able to create a model for your software. This model highlights the important aspects of the software in a clear form

© Springer International Publishing Switzerland 2015
M. Seidl et al., *UML @ Classroom*, Undergraduate Topics
in Computer Science, DOI 10.1007/978-3-319-12742-2_1

of notation that is as simple as possible but abstracts from irrelevant details, just like models in architecture, e.g., construction plans. A construction plan for a building contains information such as the floor plan. Construction materials to be used are not specified at this point in time; they are irrelevant and would make the plan more complicated than necessary. The plan also does not contain any information about how the electrical cables are to be laid. A separate plan is created for this aspect to avoid presenting too much information at once. Just like in architecture, it is important in information technology that people with different backgrounds (e.g., architect and builder) can read, interpret, and implement the model.

Modeling language   *Modeling languages* were developed precisely for such scenarios and demonstrate clearly defined rules for a structured description of a system. These languages can be *textual* (e.g., a programming language such as Java) or *visual* (e.g., a language that provides symbols for transistors, diodes, etc. that can be combined with one another). Modeling languages can be designed for a specific domain, for example, for describing web applications. On the one hand, these *domain-specific modeling languages* provide tools and guidelines for solving problems in a specific field efficiently; on the other hand, they can also be restrictive. Alternatively, modeling languages can be designed for general purpose use. The language UML, which is the subject of this book, is a general purpose modeling language. We will use UML to get to know the most important concepts of object-oriented modeling.

Object-oriented   *Object-oriented modeling* is a form of modeling that obeys the
modeling   object-oriented paradigm. In the following two subsections, we will look briefly at the notion of a model and the main concepts of object orientation. This will provide us with a good basis for our subsequent examination of object-oriented modeling with UML.

1.2 Models

System   Models allow us to describe systems efficiently and elegantly. A *system* is an integrated whole made up of components that are related to one another and influence each other in such a way that they can be perceived as a single, task-based or purpose-based unit. In this regard, they separate themselves from the surrounding environment [52]. Examples of systems are material things, such as cars or airplanes, ecological environments, such as lakes and forests, but also organizational units such as a university or a company. In information technology, we are inter-
Software system   ested in particular in software systems and thus in models that describe software systems.

Software systems themselves are based on *abstractions* that represent machine-processable facts of reality. In this context, abstraction means generalization—setting aside specific and individual features. Abstract is the opposite of concrete. Abstracting therefore means moving away from specifics, distinguishing the substance from the incidental, recognizing common characteristics [29].

Abstraction

When creating software systems, it is extremely important to select suitable means of abstraction: on the one hand for the implementation, but on the other hand also for the subsequent use of the software systems. Choosing the correct means of abstraction makes programming easier. The individual parts then have simple and small interfaces. New functionality can be introduced without the need for extensive reorganization. Choosing the wrong means of abstraction might result in a number of nasty surprises during implementation: the interfaces will be complicated and it will be difficult to implement changes. You can only manage the ever-increasing complexity of modern software systems with suitable means of abstraction [26]. This is where modeling can provide valuable services.

Selecting means of abstraction

To develop a better understanding of modeling concepts, below we present widespread and generally recognized definitions of the notion of a model as well as the properties that a good model should possess.

The notion of a *model* is important not only in information technology but also in many other scientific disciplines (mathematics, philosophy, psychology, economics, etc.). Derived from the Latin "modulus", which designates a scale in architecture, during the Renaissance the word "modello" was used in Italy for an illustrative object intended to present the form and design of a planned building to a client and to clarify design and architectural questions. Over the subsequent centuries, the notion of a "model" has been used in various branches of science for a simplified description of complex facts from reality.

Model

In 1973, Herbert Stachowiak proposed a model theory that is distinguished by three characteristics [48]:

Definition by Herbert Stachowiak

1. *Mapping:* a model is always an image (mapping) of something, a representation of natural or artificial originals that can be models themselves.
2. *Reduction:* a model does not capture all attributes of the original, rather only those that seem relevant to the modeler or user of the model.
3. *Pragmatism:* pragmatism means orientation toward usefulness. A model is assigned to an original based on the following questions: *For whom? Why? What for?* A model is used by the modeler or user instead of the original within a specific time frame and for a specific purpose.

Models support a representation of a system that is reduced to the essentials in order to minimize the complexity of the system to manageable aspects. A system is usually described not by one single view but by a number of views that together produce a unified overall picture. Thus, one view might describe the objects involved and their relationship to one another; another view might describe the behavior of a group of objects or present the interactions between different objects.

Properties of models   Models must be created with great care and due consideration. According to Bran Selic [47], five characteristics determine the quality of a model:

- *Abstraction:* a model is always a reduced representation of the system that it represents. Because the details that are irrelevant in a specific context are hidden or removed, it is easier for the user to understand the essence of the whole.
- *Understandability:* simply omitting irrelevant details is not enough to make a model understandable. It is important to present the remaining elements as intuitively as possible—for example, in a graphical notation. The understandability results directly from the expressiveness of the modeling language. Expressiveness can be defined as the ability to present complex content with as few concepts as possible. In this way, a good model reduces the intellectual effort required to understand the content depicted. For example, typical programming languages are not particularly expressive for a human reader as a lot of effort is required to understand the content of the program.
- *Accuracy:* a model must highlight the relevant properties of the real system, reflecting reality as closely as possible.
- *Predictiveness:* a model must enable prediction of interesting but not obvious properties of the system being modeled. This can be done via simulation or analysis of formal properties.
- *Cost-effectiveness:* in the long-run, it must be cheaper to create the model than to create the system being modeled.

Models can be used for various purposes. Thus we distinguish between *descriptive* and *prescriptive* models [17]. *Descriptive models* *Descriptive model* show a part of the reality to make a specific aspect easier to understand. For example, a city map describes a city in such a way as to help *Prescriptive model* a non-local person to find routes within the city. In contrast, *prescriptive models* are used to offer a construction manual for the system to be developed.

In this book, we look at how the different aspects of a software system can be modeled using a modeling language—the Unified Modeling *Executable code as* Language—such that executable code can be derived either manually *model* or (semi)automatically, or easily understandable documentation can be created. Incidentally, the executable code, developed in any programming language, such as Java, is also a model. This model represents the problem to be solved and is optimized for execution on computers.

To summarize, there are three applications for models [19]:

- Models as a sketch
- Models as a blueprint
- Models as executable programs

Models are used as a *sketch* to communicate certain aspects of a system in a simple way. Here, the model is not a complete mapping of the system. Sketches are actually distinguished by their selectivity, as they are reduced to the essential aspects for solving a problem. Sketches often make alternative solutions visible. These are then discussed in the development team. Thus, models are also used as a basis for discussion.

Models as a sketch

In contrast to the use of models as sketches, completeness is very important when models are used as a *blueprint*. These models must contain sufficient detail to enable developers to create ready-to-run systems without having to make design decisions. Models used as blueprints often do not specify the whole system, only certain parts. For example, the interface definitions between subsystems are defined in the model, whereby the developers are free to decide on the internal implementation details. If the models are behavioral descriptions, the behavior can also be simulated and tested to identify faults in advance.

Models as a blueprint

Models as sketches and blueprints can be used for both *forward engineering* and *backward engineering*. In forward engineering, the model is the basis for creating code, while in backward engineering, the model is generated from the code to document the code in a clear and easily understandable way.

Forward and backward engineering

Finally, models can be used as *executable programs*. This means that models can be specified so precisely that code can be generated from them automatically. In the context of UML, model-based software development has become extremely popular in recent years; it offers a process for using UML as a programming language. We will address this briefly in Chapter 9 of this book, after we have discussed the basics of UML. In some application areas, such as the development of embedded systems, models are already being used instead of traditional programming languages. In other areas, active research is taking place to raise the development of software systems to a new and more easily maintainable and less error-prone abstraction level.

Models as executable programs

1.3 Object Orientation

Object orientation   If we want to model in an object-oriented style, we must first clarify what *object orientation* means. The introduction of object orientation dates back to the 1960s when the simulation language SIMULA [24] was presented, building on a paradigm that was as natural to humans as possible to describe the world. The object-oriented approach corresponds to the way we look at the real world; we see it as a society of autonomous individuals, referred to as objects, which take a fixed place in this society and must thereby fulfill predefined obligations.

There is not only one single definition for object orientation. However, there is a general consensus about the properties that characterize object orientation. Naturally, objects play a central role in object-oriented approaches. Viewed simply, objects are elements in a system whose data and operations are described. Objects interact and communicate with one another. In general, we expect the concepts described below from an object-oriented approach.

1.3.1 Classes

Class   In many object-oriented approaches, it is possible to define *classes* that describe the attributes and the behavior of a set of objects (the instances of a class) abstractly and thus group common features of objects. For example, people have a name, an address, and a social security number. Courses have a unique identifier, a title, and a description. Lecture halls have a name as well as a location, etc. A class also defines a set of permitted operations that can be applied to the instances of the class. For example, you can reserve a lecture hall for a certain date, a student can register for an exam, etc. In this way, classes describe the behavior of objects.

1.3.2 Objects

Object   The instances of a class are referred to as its *objects*. For example, lh1, the Lecture Hall 1 of the Vienna University of Technology, is a concrete instance of the class LectureHall. In particular, an object is distinguished by the fact that it has its own identity, that is, different instances of a class can be uniquely identified. For example, the beamer in Lecture Hall 1 is a different object to the beamer in Lecture Hall 2, even if the devices are of the same type. Here we refer to *identical* devices but not the *same* device. The situation for concrete values of data types is different: the number 1, which is a concrete value of the data type `Integer`, does not have a distinguishable identity.

An object always has a certain state. A state is expressed by the values of its attributes. For example, a lecture hall can have the state `occupied` or `free`. An object also displays behavior. The behavior of an object is described by the set of its operations. Operations are triggered by sending a message.

1.3.3 Encapsulation

Encapsulation is the protection against unauthorized access to the internal state of an object via a uniquely defined interface. Different levels of visibility of the interfaces help to define different access authorizations. Java, for example, has the explicit visibility markers `public`, `private`, and `protected`, which respectively permit access for all, only within the object, and only for members of the same class, its subclasses, and of the same package.

Encapsulation

1.3.4 Messages

Objects communicate with one another through *messages*. A message to an object represents a request to execute an operation. The object itself decides whether and how to execute this operation. The operation is only executed if the sender is authorized to call the operation—this can be regulated in the form of visibilities (see the previous paragraph)—and a suitable implementation is available. In many object-oriented programming and modeling languages the concept of *overloading* is supported. This enables an operation to be defined differently for different types of parameters. For example, the operator + realizes different behavior depending on whether it is used to add up integers (e.g., 1 + 1 = 2) or to concatenate character strings (e.g., "a" + "b" = "ab").

Message

Overloading

1.3.5 Inheritance

The concept of *inheritance* is a mechanism for deriving new classes from existing classes. A subclass derived from an existing class (= su-

Inheritance

perclass) inherits all visible attributes and operations (specification and implementation) of the superclass. A subclass can:

- Define new attributes and/or operations
- Overwrite the implementation of inherited operations
- Add its own code to inherited operations

Class hierarchy   Inheritance enables extensible classes and as a consequence, the creation of *class hierarchies* as the basis for object-oriented system development. A class hierarchy consists of classes with similar properties, for example, Person ← Employee ← Professor ← ... where A ← B means that B is a subclass of A.

When used correctly, inheritance offers many advantages: reuse of program or model parts (thus avoiding redundancy and errors), consistent definition of interfaces, use as a modeling aid through a natural categorization of the occurring elements, and support for incremental development, i.e., a step-by-step refinement of general concepts to specific concepts.

1.3.6 Polymorphism

Polymorphism   In general terms, *polymorphism* is the ability to adopt different forms. During the execution of a program, a polymorphic attribute can have references to objects from different classes. When this attribute is declared, a type (e.g., class Person) is assigned statically at compile time. At runtime, this attribute can also be bound dynamically to a subtype (e.g., subclass Employee or subclass Student).

A polymorphic operation can be executed on objects from different classes and have different semantics in each case. This scenario can be implemented in many ways: (i) via *parametric polymorphism*, better known as genericity—here, type parameters are used. In Java for example, the concrete classes are transferred to the operations as arguments; (ii) via *inclusion polymorphism*—operations can be applied to classes and to their direct and indirect subclasses; (iii) via *overloading of operations*; and (iv) via *coercion*, that is, the conversion of types. The first two methods above are known as *universal polymorphism*; the other two methods are referred to as *ad hoc polymorphism* [13].

1.4 The Structure of the Book

In Chapter 2 we give a short overview of UML by recapitulating the history of its creation and taking a brief look at its 14 different diagrams. Then, in Chapter 3, we introduce the concepts of the use case diagram. This diagram enables us to describe the requirements that a system to be developed should satisfy. In Chapter 4 we present the class diagram. This diagram allows us to describe the structure of a system. To enable us to model the behavior of a system, in Chapter 5 we introduce the state machine diagram, in Chapter 6 the sequence diagram, and in Chapter 7 the activity diagram. We explain the interaction of the different types of diagrams in Chapter 8 with three examples. In Chapter 9, we briefly examine advanced concepts that are of significant importance for the practical use of UML.

The concepts are all explained using examples, all of which are based on the typical Austrian university environment. In most cases they represent heavily simplified scenarios. It is not our intention in this book to model one single, continuous system, as there is a high risk that in doing so we would become lost in a multitude of technical details. We have therefore selected examples according to their didactic benefit and their illustrative strength of expression. In many cases, we have therefore made assumptions that, for didactic reasons, are based on simplified presentations of reality.

UML is based entirely on object-oriented concepts. This is particularly noticeable in the class diagram, which can easily be translated into an object-oriented programming language. We will get to know the class diagram and possible translations to program code in Chapter 4. However, UML has not been designed for one specific object-oriented language. For the sake for readability, we use a notion of object-orientation as found in modern programming languages like Java or C#.

Chapter 2
A Short Tour of UML

Before introducing the most important concepts of UML in the following chapters, we first explain the background of this modeling language. We look at how UML came into being and what the "U" for "Unified" actually means. We then answer the question of how UML itself is defined, that is, where do the rules come from that dictate what a valid model should look like in UML? Furthermore, we outline what UML is used for. Finally, we give a short overview of all 14 UML diagrams in the current version 2.4.1 of the UML standard specification. These diagrams can be used for modeling both structure and behavior.

2.1 The History of UML

The introduction of object-oriented concepts in information technology originates from the work of the early 1960s [12]. The first ideas were implemented in systems such as Sketchpad, which offered a new, graphical communication approach between man and computer [28, 51].

Origins of object orientation

Today, the programming language SIMULA [24] is regarded as the first object-oriented programming language. SIMULA was primarily used to develop simulation software and was not particularly widely used. It already included concepts such as classes, objects, inheritance, and dynamic binding [2].

SIMULA

The introduction of these concepts was the start of a revolution in software development. In the subsequent decades, there followed a multitude of programming languages based on the object-oriented paradigm [21]. These included languages such as C++ [50], Eiffel [31], and Smalltalk [28]. They already contained many of the important concepts of modern programming languages and are still used today.

Object-oriented programming languages

© Springer International Publishing Switzerland 2015
M. Seidl et al., *UML @ Classroom*, Undergraduate Topics
in Computer Science, DOI 10.1007/978-3-319-12742-2_2

The emergence and introduction of object orientation as a method in software engineering is closely connected to the appearance of object-oriented programming languages. Today, object orientation is a proven and well-established approach for dealing with the complexity of software systems. It is applied not only in programming languages but also in other areas, such as in databases or the description of user interfaces.

As we have already discussed in Section 1.2, where we introduced the notion of a model, software systems are abstractions aimed at solving problems of the real world with the support of machines. Procedural programming languages are not necessarily the most appropriate tools for describing the real world: the differences in concept between a natural description of a problem and the practical implementation as a program are huge. Object-oriented programming was an attempt to develop better programs that, above all, are easier to maintain [12].

Over the years, object orientation has become the most important software development paradigm. This is reflected in object-oriented programming languages such as Java [4] or C# [32] and object-oriented modeling languages such as UML. However, the road to the current state-of-the-art of software development was long and winding.

Ada

In the 1980s, the programming language Ada, funded by the United States Department of Defense, was extremely popular due to its powerful concepts and efficient compilers [25]. Even back then, Ada supported abstract data types in the form of *packages* and concurrency in the form of *tasks*. Packages allowed the separation of specification and implementation and the usage of objects and classes of objects. Ada thus distinguished itself fundamentally from other popular languages of that time, such as Fortran and Cobol. As a consequence, there followed a great demand for object-oriented analysis and design methods to make the development of Ada programs easier. Due to the wide distribution of Ada and the pressure from the United States Department of Defense, these modeling methods were based specifically on the characteristics

Booch method

of Ada. Grady Booch was one of the first researchers to publish work on the object-oriented design of Ada programs [5].

Over time, a number of further object-oriented modeling methods arose (see [12] for an overview). In general, the modeling methods had either a strong reference to programming languages, such as the

OMT approach by Rumbaugh et al.

Booch method, or a strong reference to data modeling, such as the *Object Modeling Technique* (OMT) approach developed by James Rumbaugh et al. [42]. OMT supported the development of complex objects in the sense of an object-oriented extension of the entity-relationship model [14] which had been introduced for describing databases.

OOSE approach by Jacobson et al.

Independently of this, Ivar Jacobson et al. introduced the *Object-Oriented Software Engineering* (OOSE) approach [27]. This approach was originally developed to describe telecommunication systems.

In the 1980s and early 1990s, the modeling world was flooded with   *Method war*
a multitude of different modeling languages. Considerable effort was
required to deal with the resulting compatibility problems. The models
of different project partners were often not compatible and it was not
always possible to reuse models in different projects. The result was
exhausting discussions about different notations, which detracted from
the actual modeling problems. As new modeling languages were ap-
pearing all the time, there was no clarity about which were worthy of
investment and which were just a short-lived trend. If a language did
not become accepted, all investments that had been made to establish it
within a project or a company were generally lost. Looking back, this
time of numerous approaches, often with the difference being only in
the detail, is referred to as the *method war*.

To put an end to this unsatisfactory situation, in 1996 the *Object*   *Object Management*
Management Group (OMG) [33], the most important standardization   *Group (OMG)*
body for object-oriented software development, called for the specification of a uniform modeling standard.

In the previous year, 1995, Grady Booch, Ivar Jacobson, and James
Rumbaugh had combined their ideas and approaches at the OOPSLA
conference (OOPSLA stands for Object-Oriented Programming, Systems, Languages, and Applications). Since then, Booch, Jacobson, and
Rumbaugh have often been called the "three amigos". They set them-   *Three amigos*
selves the following objectives [1]:

- Use of object-oriented concepts to represent complete systems rather
  than just one part of the software
- Establishment of an explicit relationship between modeling concepts
  and executable program code
- Consideration of scaling factors that are inherent in complex and critical systems
- Creation of a modeling language that can be processed by machines
  but can also be read by human beings

The result of their efforts was the *Unified Modeling Language* (UML)   *Unified Modeling*
which was submitted in version 1.0 in 1997 in response to the OMG   *Language (UML)*
call. A number of former competitors were involved in the creation of
version 1.1 that subsequently appeared in 1998. One of the main objectives was a consistent specification of the language core of UML which
is documented in the *metamodel* (see Chapter 9). The metamodel de-   *Metamodel*
fines which model elements the language UML provides and how to use
them correctly. For formulating constraints which the model elements
have to fullfill, the *Object Constraint Language* (OCL) [36], based on   *Object Constraint*
predicate logic, was introduced. In subsequent versions, along with the   *Language (OCL)*
revision of certain language concepts, mechanisms for the interchange-
ability of models in the form of the *XML Metadata Interchange format*

XML Metadata Interchange format (XMI)

(XMI) [38] were added. In addition to these rather small changes, in 2000 the OMG initiated a modernization process for UML. This finally led to the adoption of the language standard UML 2.0 in 2005. With the exception of small changes which, through interim versions, resulted in the current version 2.4.1, this is the language description of UML that we will get to know and use in this book.

Today, UML is one of the most widespread graphical object-oriented modeling languages. Despite the numerous revisions, its roots (Booch method, OMT, OOSE) are still clearly recognizable. UML is suitable for modeling both complex object relationships and processes with concurrency. UML is a general purpose modeling language, meaning that its use is not restricted to a specific application area. It provides language and modeling concepts and an intuitive graphical notation for modeling various application areas, enabling a software system to be specified, designed, visualized, and documented [43]. The result of modeling with UML is a graphical model that offers different views of a system in the form of various diagrams.

2.2 Usage

UML is not tied to a specific development tool, specific programming language, or specific target platform on which the system to be developed must be used. Neither does UML offer a software development process. UML in fact separates the modeling language and modeling method. The latter can be defined on a project-specific or company-specific basis. However, the language concepts of UML do favor an iterative and incremental process [43].

Use in the software development process

UML can be used consistently across the entire software development process. At all stages of development, the same language concepts can be used in the same notation. Thus, a model can be refined in stages. There is no need for a model to be translated into another modeling language. This enables an iterative and incremental software development process. UML is well-suited for various application areas with different requirements regarding complexity, data volume, real time, etc.

Generic language concepts

Semantic variation point

The UML model elements and their correct use are specified in the UML *metamodel* [35]. The language concepts are defined so generically that a wide and flexible applicability is achieved. To avoid restricting the use of UML, the standard is (intentionally) vague at various points, permitting different interpretations in the form of semantic variation points. However, this is a two-edged sword; it also leads to different implementations of the language standard by modeling tools, which in turn, unfortunately makes it difficult to exchange models.

2.3 Diagrams

In UML, a model is represented graphically in the form of *diagrams*. A diagram provides a view of that part of reality described by the model. There are diagrams that express which users use which functionality and diagrams that show the structure of the system but without specifying a concrete implementation. There are also diagrams that represent supported and forbidden processes. In the current version 2.4.1, UML offers 14 diagrams that describe either the structure or the behavior of a system.

Diagram

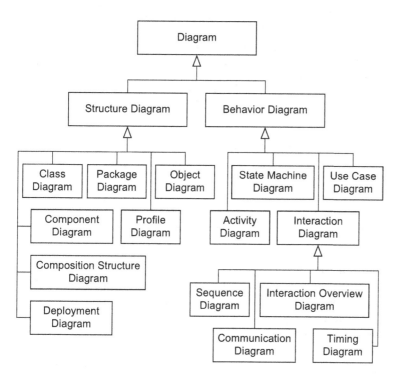

Figure 2.1
UML diagrams

Figure 2.1 shows a taxonomy of the 14 UML diagrams [35], giving a very rough categorization. As the figure shows, we differentiate between *structure diagrams* and *behavior diagrams*. The behavior diagrams include the interaction diagrams, which in turn consist of four diagrams (see Chapter 6).

A diagram is usually enclosed by a rectangle with a pentagon in the top left-hand corner. This pentagon contains the diagram type and the name of the diagram. Optionally, parameters may be specified following the name which then can be used within the diagram. Figure 2.2 con-

Notation for diagram frame

Figure 2.2

Examples of UML diagram frames

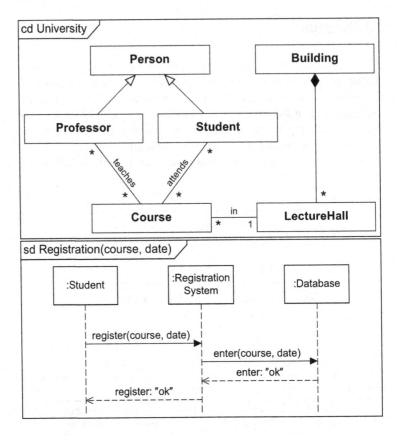

tains two examples of diagram frames. In particular, it shows a class diagram (cd) with the name University and a sequence diagram (sd) called Registration with the parameters course and date.

Note   A concept that may occur in all diagrams is the *note*. A note can contain any form of expression that specifies the diagram and its elements more precisely—for example, in natural language or in the Object Constraint Language (OCL). Notes may be attached to all other model elements. Figure 2.3 shows an example of the use of a note which specifies in natural language that persons are not permitted to grade themselves. The class Person and the association grades represent concepts of the class diagram that will be introduced in Chapter 4.

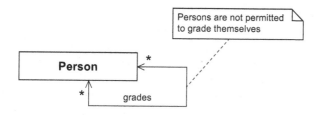

Figure 2.3
Example of a note

2.3.1 Structure Diagrams

UML offers seven types of diagrams for modeling the structure of a system from different perspectives. The dynamic behavior of the elements in question (i.e., their changes over time) is not considered in these diagrams.

The Class Diagram

Just like the concepts of the object diagram (see next paragraph), the concepts of the *class diagram* originate from conceptual data modeling and object-oriented software development. These concepts are used to specify the data structures and object structures of a system. The class diagram is based primarily on the concepts of *class*, *generalization*, and *association*. For example, in a class diagram, you can model that the classes Course, Student, and Professor occur in a system. Professors teach courses and students attend courses. Students and professors have common properties as they are both members of the class Person. This is expressed by a generalization relationship.

*Class diagram
(see Chapter 4)*

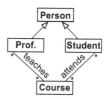

The Object Diagram

Based on the definitions of the related class diagram, an *object diagram* shows a concrete snapshot of the system state at a specific execution time. For example, an object diagram could show that a professor Henry Foster (henryFoster) teaches the courses Object-Oriented Modeling (oom) and Object-Oriented Programming (oop).

*Object diagram
(see Chapter 4)*

The Package Diagram

Package diagram

The *package diagram* groups diagrams or model elements according to common properties, such as functional cohesion. For example, in a university administration system, you could introduce packages that contain information about the teaching, the research, and the administrative aspects. Packages are often integrated in other diagrams rather than being shown in separate diagrams.

The Component Diagram

Component diagram

UML pays homage to component-oriented software development by offering *component diagrams*. A component is an independent, executable unit that provides other components with services or uses the services of other components. UML does not prescribe any strict separation between object-oriented and component-oriented concepts. Indeed, these concepts may be combined in any way required. When specifying a component, you can model two views explicitly: the external view (black box view), which represents the specification of the component, and the internal view (white box view), which defines the implementation of the component.

The Composition Structure Diagram

Composition structure diagram

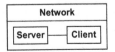

The *composition structure diagram* allows a hierarchical decomposition of the parts of the system. You can therefore use a composition structure diagram to describe the internal structure of classes or components in detail. This enables you to achieve a higher level of detail than, for example, in a class diagram because the modeling is context-specific. You can specify details of the internal structure that are valid precisely for the context under consideration.

The Deployment Diagram

Deployment diagram

The hardware topology used and the runtime system assigned can be represented by the *deployment diagram*. The hardware encompasses processing units in the form of nodes as well as communication relationships between the nodes. A runtime system contains artifacts that are deployed to the nodes.

The Profile Diagram

Using *profiles*, you can extend UML to introduce domain-specific con- *Profile diagram*
cepts. The actual core of the language definition of UML, the meta-
model, remains unchanged. You can thus reuse modeling tools without
having to make adjustments. For example, you can use profiles to introduce the concept of Java Enterprise Beans.

«metaclass»
Component

«stereotype»
Bean

2.3.2 Behavior Diagrams

With the *behavior diagrams*, UML offers the infrastructure that enables
you to define behavior in detail.

Behavior refers to the direct consequences of an action of at least one
object. It affects how the states of objects change over time. Behavior
can either be specified through the actions of a single object or result
from interactions between multiple objects.

The Use Case Diagram

UML offers the *use case diagram* to enable you to define the require- *Use case diagram*
ments that a system must fulfill. This diagram describes which users use *(see Chapter 3)*
which functionalities of the system but does not address specific details
of the implementation. The units of functionality that the system provides for its users are called *use cases*. In a university administration
system, for example, the functionality Registration would be a use case
used by students.

Administration

Registration

Student

The State Machine Diagram

Within their life cycle, objects go through different states. For example, *State machine diagram*
a person is in the state logged out when first visiting a website. The state *(see Chapter 5)*
changes to logged in after the person successfully entered username and
password (event login). As soon as the person logs out (event logout), the
person returns to the state logged out. This behavior can be represented
in UML using the *state machine diagram*. This diagram describes the
permissible behavior of an object in the form of possible states and state
transitions triggered by various events.

The Activity Diagram

Activity diagram
(see Chapter 7)

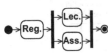

You can model processes of any kind using *activity diagrams*: both business processes and software processes. For example, an activity diagram can show which actions are necessary for a student to participate in a lecture and an assignment. Activity diagrams offer control flow mechanisms as well as data flow mechanisms that coordinate the actions that make up an activity, that is, a process.

The Sequence Diagram

Sequence diagram
(see Chapter 6)

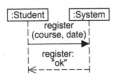

The *sequence diagram* describes the interactions between objects to fulfill a specific task, for example, registration for an exam in a university administration system. The focus is on the chronological order of the messages exchanged between the interaction partners. Various constructs for controlling the chronological order of the messages as well as concepts for modularization allow you to model complex interactions.

The Communication Diagram

Communication diagram
(see Chapter 6)

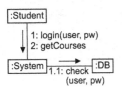

Similarly to the sequence diagram, the *communication diagram* describes the communication between different objects. Here, the focus is on the communication relationships between the interaction partners rather than on the chronological order of the message exchange. Complex control structures are not available. This diagram clearly shows who interacts with whom.

The Timing Diagram

Timing diagram
(see Chapter 6)

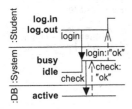

The *timing diagram* explicitly shows the state changes of the interaction partners that can occur due to time events or as a result of the exchange of messages. For example, a person is in the state logged in as soon as the message is received from the university administration system that the password sent is valid.

The Interaction Overview Diagram

The *interaction overview diagram* models the connection between different interaction processes by setting individual interaction diagrams (i.e., sequence diagram, communication diagram, timing diagram, and other interaction overview diagrams) in a time-based and causal sequence. It also specifies conditions under which interaction processes are permitted to take place. To model the control flow, concepts from the activity diagram are used. For example, a user of the university administration system must first log in (which already represents a separate interaction with the system) before being allowed to use further functionalities.

Interaction overview diagram
(see Chapter 6)

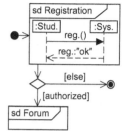

2.4 Diagrams Presented in this Book

As already explained in Chapter 1, this book restricts itself to the five most important and most widespread types of UML diagrams, namely the use case diagram, class diagram (including the object diagram), state machine diagram, sequence diagram, and activity diagram. In this book, we present these diagrams in the order in which they would generally be used in software development projects. We begin with the use case diagram, which specifies the basic functionality of a software system. The class diagram then defines which objects or which classes are involved in the realization of this functionality. The state machine diagram then defines the intra-object behavior, while the sequence diagram specifies the inter-object behavior. Finally, the activity diagram allows us to define those processes that "implement" the use cases from the use case diagram.

Chapter 3
The Use Case Diagram

The *use case diagram* allows us to describe the possible usage scenarios (use cases) that a system is developed for. It expresses what a system should do but does not address any realization details such as data structures, algorithms, etc. These details are covered by other diagrams such as the class diagram (see Chapter 4) or the interaction diagrams (see Chapter 6). The use case diagram also models which user of the system uses which functionality, i.e., it expresses who will actually work with the system to be built.

Use case diagram

The *use case* is a fundamental concept of many object-oriented development methods. It is applied during the entire analysis and design process. Use cases represent what the customer wants the system to do, that is, the customer's requirements of the system. At a very high abstraction level, the use cases show what the future system is for. A use case diagram can also be used to document the functionality of an existing system and to record retrospectively which users are permitted to use which functionality.

Specifically, we can employ a use case diagram to answer the following questions:

1. What is being described? (*The system.*)
2. Who interacts with the system? (*The actors.*)
3. What can the actors do? (*The use cases.*)

The use case diagram provides only a few language elements. At first glance, this diagram seems to be extremely simple to learn and use. In practice, however, the use case diagram is an extremely underestimated diagram. The content of a use case diagram express the expectations that the customer has of the system to be developed. The diagram documents the requirements the system should fulfill. This is essential for a detailed technical design. If use cases are forgotten or specified imprecisely or

© Springer International Publishing Switzerland 2015
M. Seidl et al., *UML @ Classroom*, Undergraduate Topics
in Computer Science, DOI 10.1007/978-3-319-12742-2_3

incorrectly, in some circumstances the consequences can be extremely
serious: the development and maintenance costs increase, the users are
dissatisfied, etc. As a consequence, the system is used less successfully
and the investments made in the development of the system do not bring
the expected returns. Even though software engineering and methods of
requirements analysis are not the subject of this book, we briefly explain
why it is essential to create use cases very carefully. Furthermore, we
discuss where errors are often made and how these can be avoided with
a systematic approach. For a detailed introduction to these topics, see
for example [3, 45].

3.1 Use Cases

Use case

Trigger

A *use case* describes functionality expected from the system to be developed. It encompasses a number of functions that are executed when
using this system. A use case provides a tangible benefit for one or more
actors that communicate with this use case. The use case diagram does
not cover the internal structure and the actual implementation of a use
case. In general, a use case is triggered either by invocation of an actor
or by a *trigger event*, in short, a *trigger*. An example of a trigger is that
the semester has ended and hence the use case Issue certificate must be
executed.

Use cases are determined by collecting customer wishes and analyzing problems specified in natural language when these are the basis
for the requirements analysis. However, use cases can also be used to
document the functionality that a system offers. A use case is usually
represented as an ellipse. The name of the use case is specified directly
in or directly beneath the ellipse. Alternatively, a use case can be represented by a rectangle that contains the name of the use case in the
center and a small ellipse in the top right-hand corner. The different notation alternatives for the use case Query student data are illustrated in
Figure 3.1. The alternatives are all equally valid, but the first alternative, the ellipse that contains the name of the use case, is the one most
commonly used.

Figure 3.1
Notation alternatives for
use cases

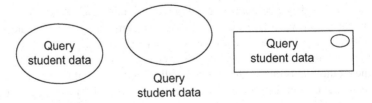

The set of all use cases together describes the functionality that a software system provides. The use cases are generally grouped within a rectangle. This rectangle symbolizes the boundaries of the *system* to be described. The example in Figure 3.2 shows the Student Administration system, which offers three use cases: (1) Query student data, (2) Issue certificate, and (3) Announce exam. These use cases may be triggered by the actor Professor.

System

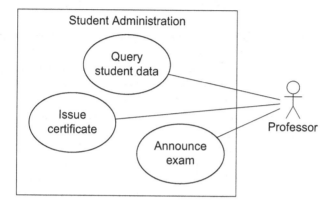

Figure 3.2
Representation of system boundaries

3.2 Actors

To describe a system completely, it is essential to document not only what the system can do but also who actually works and interacts with the system. In the use case diagram, *actors* always interact with the system in the context of their use cases, that is, the use cases with which they are associated. The example in Figure 3.2 contains only the actor Professor, who can query student data, announce exams, and issue certificates. Actors are represented by stick figures, rectangles (containing the additional information «actor»), or by a freely definable symbol. The notation alternatives are shown in Figure 3.3. These three notation alternatives are all equally valid. As we can see from this example, actors can be *human* (e.g., student or professor) or *non-human* (e.g., e-mail server). The symbols used to represent the actors in a specific use case diagram depend on the person creating the model or the tool used. Note in particular that non-human actors can also be portrayed as stick figures, even if this seems counterintuitive.

Actor

X

Figure 3.3
Notation alternatives for
actors

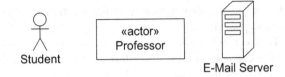

Student   **E-Mail Server**

Types of actors:

- *Human/non-human*
- *Active/passive*
- *Primary/
  secondary*

An actor interacts with the system by using the system as an *active* actor, meaning that the actor initiates the execution of use cases; alternatively, the interaction involves the actor being used by the system, meaning that the actor is a *passive* actor providing functionality for the execution of use cases. In example (a) in Figure 3.4, the actor Professor is an active actor, whereas the actor E-Mail Server is passive. However, both are required for the execution of the use case Inform student. Furthermore, use case diagrams can also contain both *primary* and *secondary* actors, also shown in this example. A primary actor takes an actual benefit from the execution of the use case (in our example this is the Professor), whereas the the secondary actor E-Mail Server receives no direct benefit from the execution of the use case. As we can see in example (b) in Figure 3.4, the secondary actor does not necessarily have to be passive. Both the Professor and the Student are actively involved in the execution of the use case Exam, whereby the main beneficiary is the Student. In contrast, the Professor has a lower benefit from the exam but is necessary for the execution of the use case. Graphically, there is no differentiation between primary and secondary actors, between active and passive actors, and between human and non-human actors.

Figure 3.4
Examples of actors

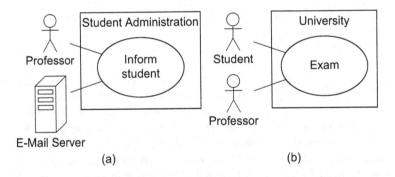

(a)   (b)

An actor is always clearly outside the system, i.e., a user is never part of the system and is therefore never implemented. Data about the user, however, can be available within the system and can be represented, for example, by a class in a class diagram (see Chapter 4). Sometimes it is difficult to decide whether an element is part of the system to be imple-

mented or serves as an actor. In example (a) in Figure 3.4, the E-Mail
Server is an actor—it is not part of the system but it is necessary for the
execution of the use case Inform student. However, if no external server
is required to execute this use case because the student administration
system implements the e-mail functionality itself or has its own server,
the E-Mail Server is no longer an actor. In that case, only the Professor is
required to inform students about various news items.

3.3 Associations

In the examples in Figure 3.4, we connected the actors with use cases via
solid lines without explaining this in more detail. An actor is connected
with the use cases via *associations* which express that the actor communicates with the system and uses a certain functionality. Every actor
must communicate with at least one use case. Otherwise, we would have
an actor that does not interact with the system. In the same way, every
use case must be in a relationship with at least one actor. If this were
not the case, we would have modeled a functionality that is not used by
anyone and is therefore irrelevant.

Association

An association is always binary, meaning that it is always specified
between one use case and one actor. Multiplicities may be specified
for the association ends. If a multiplicity greater than 1 is specified for
the actor's association end, this means that more than one instance of
an actor is involved in the execution of the use case. If we look at the
example in Figure 3.5, one to three students and precisely one assistant
is involved in the execution of the use case Conduct oral exam. If no
multiplicity is specified for the actor's association end, 1 is assumed as
the default value. The multiplicity at the use case's association end is
mostly unrestricted and is therefore only rarely specified explicitly.

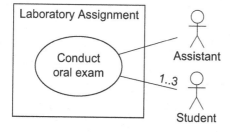

Figure 3.5
Multiplicities in
associations

Role   Actors do not represent a specific user—they represent *roles* that users adopt. If a user has adopted the respective role, this user is authorized to execute the use cases associated with this role. Specific users can adopt and set aside multiple roles simultaneously. For example, a person can be involved in the submission of a certain assignment as an assistant and in another assignment as a student. The role concept is also used in other types of UML diagrams, such as the class diagram (see Chapter 4), the sequence diagram (see Chapter 6), and the activity diagram (see Chapter 7).

3.4 Relationships between Actors

Synonyms:

● *Generalization*
● *Inheritance*

Generalization for actors

Actors often have common properties and some use cases can be used by various actors. For example, it is possible that not only professors but also assistants (i.e., the entire research personnel) are permitted to view student data. To express this, actors may be depicted in an *inheritance relationship* (generalization) with one another. When an actor Y (sub-actor) inherits from an actor X (super-actor), Y is involved with all use cases with which X is involved. In simple terms, generalization expresses an "is a" relationship. It is represented with a line from the sub-

Figure 3.6
Example of generalization
for actors

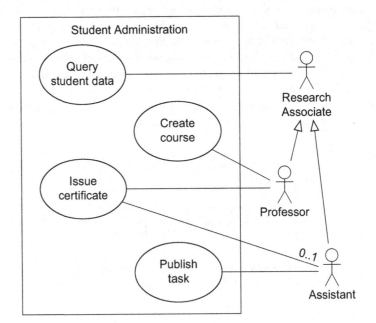

actor to the super-actor with a large triangular arrowhead at the super-actor end. In the example in Figure 3.6, the actors Professor and Assistant inherit from the actor Research Associate, which means that every professor and every assistant is a research associate. Every research associate can execute the use case Query student data. Only professors can create a new course (use case Create course); in contrast, tasks can only be published by assistants (use case Publish task). To execute the use case Issue certificate in Figure 3.6, an actor Professor is required; in addition, an actor Assistant can be involved optionally, which is expressed by the multiplicity 0..1.

There is a great difference between two actors participating in a use case themselves and two actors having a common super-actor that participates in the use case. In the first case, both actors must participate in the use case (see Fig. 3.7(a)); in the second case, each of them inherits the association. Then each actor participates in the use case individually (see Fig. 3.7(b)).

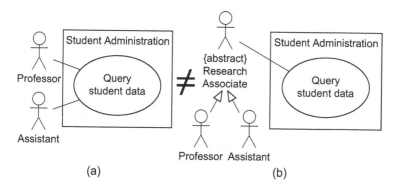

Figure 3.7
Example with and without generalization

If there is no instance of an actor, this actor can be labeled with the keyword {abstract}. Alternatively, the names of abstract actors can be represented in italic font. The actor Research Associate in Figure 3.7(b) is an example of an abstract actor. It is required to express that either a Professor or an Assistant is involved in the use case Query student data. The use of abstract actors only makes sense in the context of an inheritance relationship: the common properties of the sub-actors are grouped and described at one point, namely with the common, abstract super-actor.

Abstract actor

Generalization is a fundamental concept of object orientation and can be applied to many different language elements of UML. For a more detailed introduction to generalization, see Chapter 4.

3.5 Relationships between Use Cases

Up to this point, we have learned only about relationships between use cases and actors (associations) and between actors themselves (generalization of actors). Use cases can also be in a relationship with other use cases. Here we differentiate between «include» relationships, «extend» relationships, and generalizations of use cases.

Figure 3.8
Example of «include» and «extend»

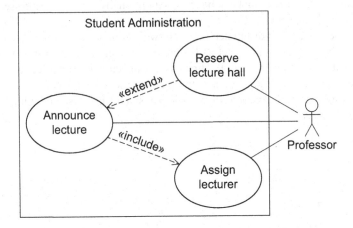

«include»

If a use case A includes a use case B, represented as a dashed arrow from A to B labeled with the keyword «include», the behavior of B is integrated into the behavior of A. Here, A is referred to as the *base use case* and B as the *included use case*. The base use case always requires the behavior of the included use case to be able to offer its functionality. In contrast, the included use case can be executed on its own. The use of «include» is analogous to calling a subroutine in a procedural programming language. In the use case diagram in Figure 3.8, the use cases Announce lecture and Assign lecturer are in an «include» relationship, whereby Announce lecture is the base use case. Therefore, whenever a new lecture is announced, the use case Assign lecturer must also be executed. The actor Professor is involved in the execution of both use cases. Further lecturers can also be assigned to an existing lecture as the included use case can be executed independently of the base use case. One use case may include multiple other use cases. One use case may also be included by multiple different use cases. In such situations, it is important to ensure that no cycle arises.

If a use case B is in an «extend» relationship with a use case A, then A can use the behavior of B but does not have to. Use case B can therefore be activated by A in order to insert the behavior of B in A. Here,

A is again referred to as the *base use case* and B as the *extending use case*. An «extend» relationship is shown with a dashed arrow from the extending use case B to the base use case A. Both use cases can also be executed independently of one another. If we look at the example in Figure 3.8, the two use cases Announce lecture and Reserve lecture hall are in an «extend» relationship. When a new lecture is announced, it is possible (but not mandatory) to reserve a lecture hall. A use case can act as an extending use case several times or can itself be extended by several use cases. Again, no cycles may arise. Note that the arrow indicating an «extend» relationship points towards the base use case, whereas the arrow indicating an «include» relationship originates from the base use case and points towards the included use case.

«extend»

A *condition* that must be fulfilled for the base use case to insert the behavior of the extending use case can be specified for every «extend» relationship. The condition is specified, within curly brackets, in a note that is connected with the corresponding «extend» relationship. A condition is indicated by the preceding keyword Condition followed by a colon. Two examples are shown in Figure 3.9. Within the context of the use case Announce lecture, a lecture hall can only be reserved if it is free. Furthermore, an exam can only be created if the required data has been entered.

Condition

By using *extension points*, you can define the point at which the behavior of the extending use cases must be inserted in the base use case. The extension points are written directly within the use case, as illustrated in the use case Announce lecture in the example in Figure 3.9. Within the use case symbol, the extension points have a separate sec-

Extension point

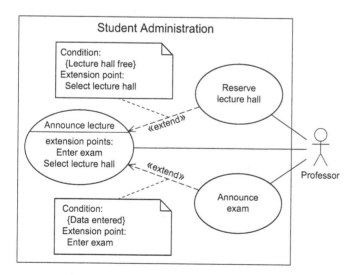

Figure 3.9
Example of extension points and conditions

tion that is identified by the keyword extension points. If a use case has multiple extension points, these can be assigned to the corresponding «extend» relationship via specification in a note similarly to a condition.

Generalization for use cases

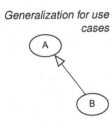

In the same way as for actors, *generalization* is also possible between use cases. Thus, common properties and common behavior of different use cases can be grouped in a parent use case. If a use case A generalizes a use case B, B inherits the behavior of A, which B can either extend or overwrite. Then, B also inherits all relationships from A. Therefore, B adopts the basic functionality of A but decides itself what part of A is executed or changed. If a use case is labeled {abstract}, it cannot be executed directly; only the specific use cases that inherit from the abstract use case are executable.

The use case diagram in Figure 3.10 shows an example of the generalization of use cases. The abstract use case Announce event passes on its properties and behavior to the use cases Announce lecture and Announce talk. As a result of an «include» relationship, both use cases must execute the behavior of the use case Assign lecturer. When a lecture is announced, an exam can also be announced at the same time. Both use cases inherit the relationship from the use case Announce event to the actor Professor. Thus, all use cases are connected to at least one actor, the prerequisite previously stipulated for correct use case diagrams.

Figure 3.10
Example of generalization of use cases

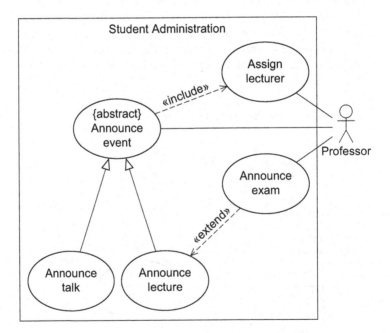

Generalization allows us to group the common features of the two use cases Announce lecture and Announce talk. This means that we do not have to model both the «include» relationship and the association with the professor twice.

3.6 Examples of Relationships

To explain again explicitly how the different relationship types in a use case diagram interact with one another, let us take a look at the use case diagram from Figure 3.11 and discuss some interesting cases that occur here.

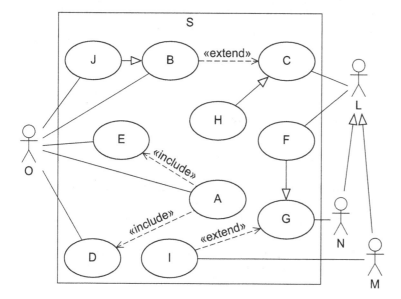

Figure 3.11
Examples of relationships in a use case diagram

- *The use case A includes the use cases E and D.* An actor O is involved in all three use cases. There is no specification of whether this is the same user or different users, that is, different instances of O.
- *The use case H inherits from the use case C.* As use case C is executed by the actor L, an actor L must also be involved in the execution of H. The actors N and M inherit from L. Therefore, both use cases C and H can also be executed by an actor M or N.

- *The use case J inherits from the use case B.* As a result of the inheritance relationship, an actor O is involved in the execution of use case J. However, an association with O is also modeled for J directly. The consequence of this is that two actors in the role O are involved in the execution of J. Note that these two actors can coincide.
- *The use case F inherits from the use case G.* As a result of the inheritance relationship, an actor N is involved in the execution of use case F. For F, an association with the actor L is also modeled directly. Therefore, an actor N and, due to the inheritance relationship of the actors L, N, and M, either an actor L or an actor M or an additional actor N is involved in the execution of F. If two actors N are involved, they may coincide.
- *The use case I extends the use case F.* As use case F inherits from use case G and as I extends use case G, this relationship is passed on to F. If G and I were in an «include» relationship, this relationship would also be passed on to F in the same way.
- *The use case J extends the use case H.* This is as a result of the inheritance relationships from B to J and from C to H.

3.7 Creating a Use Case Diagram

So, how do you create a use case diagram? First you must identify actors and use cases and then place them in relationships with one another. You then describe the use cases in detail. At first glance, this diagram seems to be simple due to the low number of concepts involved. But in fact, use case diagrams are often created incorrectly with a lot of errors. Therefore, here we take a brief look at the principles of creating use cases. For details, see the extensive literature on requirements engineering, for example [16, 30, 40]. We then explain some typical pitfalls to be avoided when modeling use case diagrams.

3.7.1 Identifying Actors and Use Cases

According to [30], there are two ways to identify use cases for prospective system design:

1. Analysis of requirements documents
2. Analysis of the expectations of future users

Requirements documents are generally natural language specifications that explain what the customer expects from a system. They should document relatively precisely who will use the system and how they will use it. If you follow the second approach for finding use cases, you must first identify the future users—that is, the actors. To identify the actors that appear in a use case diagram, you must answer the following questions:

- Who uses the main use cases? *Questions for identifying*
- Who needs support for their daily work? *actors*
- Who is responsible for system administration?
- What are the external devices/(software) systems with which the system must communicate?
- Who has an interest in the results of the system?

Once you know the actors, you can derive the use cases by asking the following questions about the actors [27]:

- What are the main tasks that an actor must perform? *Questions for identifying*
- Does an actor want to query or even modify information contained *use cases* in the system?
- Does an actor want to inform the system about changes in other systems?
- Should an actor be informed about unexpected events within the system?

In many cases, you model use cases iteratively and incrementally. In *Iterative and incremental* doing so, you often start with the "top level" requirements that reflect *determination of use* the business objectives to be pursued with the software. You then con- *cases* tinue to refine them until, at a technical level, you have specified what the system should be able to do. For example, a "top level" requirement for a university administration system could be that the system can be used for student administration. If we refine this requirement, we define that new students should be able to register at the university and enroll for studies, that the students' grades for different courses should be stored, etc.

3.7.2 Describing Use Cases

To ensure that even large use case diagrams remain clear, it is extremely important to select short, concise names for the use cases. When situations arise in which the intention behind the use case and its interpretation are not clear, you must also describe the use cases. Again, it is important to ensure that you describe the use cases clearly and concisely, as otherwise there is a risk that readers will only skim over the document.

A generally recognized guideline for the length of use case descriptions is approx. 1–2 pages per use case. In [15], Alistair Cockburn presents a structured approach for the description of use cases that contains the following information:

- Name
- Short description
- Precondition: prerequisite for successful execution
- Postcondition: system state after successful execution
- Error situations: errors relevant to the problem domain
- System state on the occurrence of an error
- Actors that communicate with the use case
- Trigger: events which initiate/start the use case
- Standard process: individual steps to be taken
- Alternative processes: deviations from the standard process

Table 3.1
Use case description for
Reserve lecture hall

Name:	Reserve lecture hall
Short description:	An employee reserves a lecture hall at the university for an event.
Precondition:	The employee is authorized to reserve lecture halls. Employee is logged in to the system.
Postcondition:	A lecture hall is reserved.
Error situations:	There is no free lecture hall.
System state in the event of an error:	The employee has not reserved a lecture hall.
Actors:	Employee
Trigger:	Employee requires a lecture hall.
Standard process:	(1) Employee selects the lecture hall. (2) Employee selects the date. (3) System confirms that the lecture hall is free. (4) Employee confirms the reservation.
Alternative processes:	(3') Lecture hall is not free. (4') System proposes an alternative lecture hall. (5') Employee selects the alternative lecture hall and confirms the reservation.

Table 3.1 contains the description of the use case Reserve lecture hall in a student administration system. The description is extremely simplified but fully sufficient for our purposes. The standard process and the alternative process could be refined further or other error situations and alternative processes could be considered. For example, it could be possible to reserve a lecture hall where an event is already taking place—this makes sense if the event is an exam that could be held in the lecture hall along with another exam, meaning that fewer exam supervisors are required. In a real project, the details would come from the requirements and wishes of the customers.

3.7.3 Pitfalls

Unfortunately, errors are often made when creating use case diagrams. Six examples of typical types of errors are discussed below. For a more detailed treatment of this topic, see [39].

Error 1: Modeling processes

Even if it is often very tempting to model entire (business) processes or workflows in a use case diagram, this is an incorrect use of the diagram. Let us assume we are modeling the system Student Office (see the final example of this chapter on page 42). If a student uses the function Collect certificate, the student must first be notified that the certificate is ready for collection in the student office. Naturally, the lecturer must have sent the certificate to the student office, i.e., the certificate has been issued. The use cases Collect certificate, Send notification, and Issue certificate may be connected chronologically but this should not be represented in a use case diagram. It is therefore incorrect to relate these use cases to one another using «include» or «extend» relationships as shown in Figure 3.12. The functionality that one of these use cases offers is not part of the functionality that another use case offers, hence the use cases must be used independently of one another.

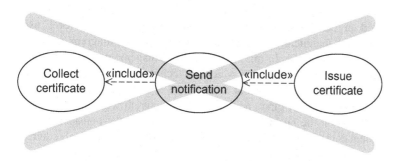

Figure 3.12
Incorrect excerpt of a use case diagram: modeling processes

Error 2: Setting system boundaries incorrectly

When modeling a use case diagram, you must consider very carefully where to draw the boundaries of the diagram. As already mentioned, this is often not clear. Actors are always outside the system boundaries: if they are to be located within the system, they are part of the system and therefore they *must not* be modeled as actors. In Figure 3.13, the Employee is depicted within the boundaries of the system Student Administration. Of course the student administration system includes employees. However, as we want to create a use case diagram of this system, we must consider whether we want to view these employees as actors or as part of the student administration system. If they are a part of the system, they must not be modeled as actors. In that case, some other entity outside the system should be an actor. If they are not part of the system but are necessary for the execution of the use cases, they must be represented as actors—outside the system boundaries.

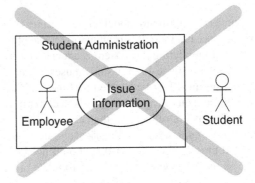

Error 3: Mixing abstraction levels

When identifying use cases, you must always ensure that they are located on the same abstraction level. Avoid representing "top level" use cases with technically oriented use cases in the same diagram, as is the case in Figure 3.14. In this example, the management of student data and the selection of a printer, which is a technical feature of the system, are shown together. To avoid this type of error, you should therefore proceed iteratively. First create a use case diagram with use cases that are based on the business objectives (in our example, management of student data). Then refine these use cases down to the technical requirements (selecting a printer).

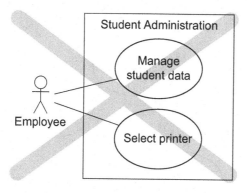

Figure 3.14
Incorrect excerpt of a use
case diagram: mixing ab-
straction levels

Error 4: Functional decomposition

Use cases—even included or extending use cases—can always be executed independently. If they can only be executed within the scope of
another use case and not independently, they are not use cases and must
not be depicted as such. Their functionality must then be covered in the
description of the use case that uses them. In Figure 3.15(a), the use
case Issue certificate is broken down into the individual subfunctions
necessary to execute the use case. These subfunctions are modeled as
use cases even though sometimes they are not meaningful independent
use cases, such as Enter data.

The use case Log in is also not a functionality that is part of Issue
certificate. In fact, it is a precondition that the user must be logged in
with sufficient authorizations for being able to execute this use case.
Therefore, a reduced use case diagram, as shown in Figure 3.15(b), is
sufficient. The other information specified in Figure 3.15(a) must be
specified in the use case description.

Error 5: Incorrect associations

If a use case is associated with two actors, this does not mean that either
one or the other actor is involved in the execution of the use case: it
means that both are necessary for its execution. In the use case diagram
in Figure 3.16(a), the actors Assistant and Professor are involved in the
execution of the use case Issue information, which is not the intention. To
resolve this problem, we can introduce a new, abstract actor Research
Associate from which the two actors Assistant and Professor inherit. The
actor Employee is now connected with the use case Issue information (see
Fig. 3.16(b)).

Figure 3.15
Incorrect excerpt of a use
case diagram: functional
decomposition

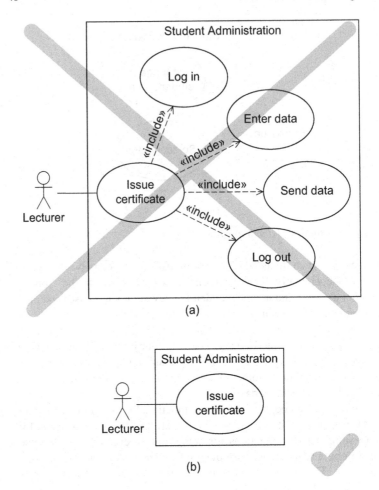

Error 6: Modeling redundant use cases

When modeling use cases, it is very tempting to create a separate use
case for each possible situation. For example, in the use case diagram in
Figure 3.17(a), we have modeled separate use cases for creating, updat-
ing, and deleting courses. This shows the different options available for
editing a course in the system. In such a small use case diagram as that
shown in Figure 3.17(a), it is not a problem to show the differentiations
at such a detailed level.

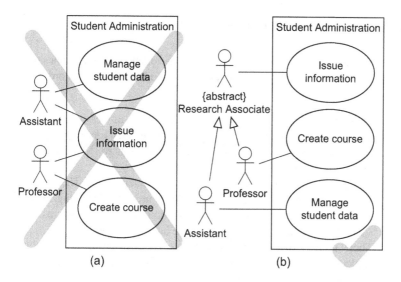

Figure 3.16
Incorrect excerpt of a use
case diagram: incorrect
associations

However, when modeling a real application, the diagram would very quickly become unmanageable. To counteract this, it might make sense to group use cases that have the same objective, namely the management of a course. This is reflected in Figure 3.17(b). The individual steps are then specified in the description of the standard process.

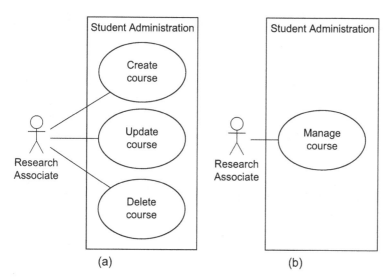

Figure 3.17
Modeling redundant use
cases

3.7.4 A Final Example

To conclude this chapter, we create a use case diagram that describes the functionality of the information system of a student office in accordance with the following specification:

- Many important administrative activities of a university are processed by the student office. Students can register for studies (matriculation), enroll, and withdraw from studies here. Matriculation involves enrolling, that is, registering for studies.
- Students receive their certificates from the student office. The certificates are printed out by an employee. Lecturers send grading information to the student office. The notification system then informs the students automatically that a certificate has been issued.
- There is a differentiation between two types of employees in the student office: a) those that are exclusively occupied with the administration of student data (service employee, or ServEmp), and b) those that fulfill the remaining tasks (administration employee, or AdminEmp), whereas all employees (ServEmp and AdminEmp) can issue information.
- Administration employees issue certificates when the students come to collect them. Administration employees also create courses. When creating courses, they can reserve lecture halls.

To create a use case diagram from this simplified specification, we first identify the actors and their relationships to one another. We then determine the use cases and their relationships to one another. Finally, we associate the actors with their use cases.

1. *Identifying actors*

If we look at the textual specification, we can identify five potential actors: Lecturer, Student, employees of the types ServEmp and AdminEmp, as well as the Notification System. As both types of employees demonstrate common behavior, namely issuing information, it makes sense to introduce a common super-actor StudOfficeEmp from which ServEmp and AdminEmp inherit. We assume that the Notification System is not part of the student office, hence we include it in the list of actors. Figure 3.18 summarizes the actors in our example.

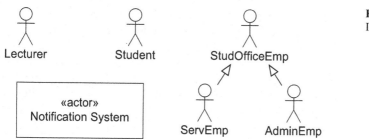

Figure 3.18
Identified actors

2. *Identifying use cases*

In the next step, we identify the use cases (see Fig. 3.19). In doing so, we determine which functionalities the student office must fulfill.

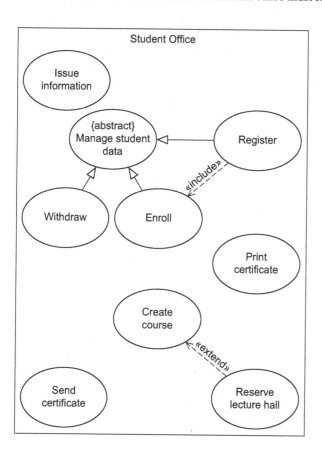

Figure 3.19
Identified use cases

The specification is very short. However, we know that the objective is to model the information system supporting the employees of a student office rather than modeling the functionalities the student office provides for the students. If we were to model the latter, we would need a use case Collect certificate, for example, in which a student would be involved. This use case is not included in the information system as it is not related to the collection of the certificates. The use case Print certificate is, however. To print, naturally we need a printer. Should we add this to our list of actors? We do not do this as we consider the printer to be an integral part of the system to be modeled.

We also have the functions Register, Enroll, and Withdraw. We could group these in one use case Manage student data as they are all performed by an actor ServEmp. In doing so, however, we would lose the information that matriculation includes enrollment for studies. Therefore, we do not reduce the three use cases to one use case. We express the relationship between Register and Enroll with an «include» relationship. As the three use cases have the association to ServEmp in common, we still introduce the use case Manage student data and model that the use cases Register, Enroll, and Withdraw inherit from this use case. To express that this use case cannot be instantiated, we define it as an abstract use case.

Lecturers can execute the use case Send certificate. If a certificate is sent to the student office, the student affected is notified. However, we do not model a separate use case Notify student as, according to the specification above, students are only notified in the context of the use case Send certificate. If Notify student cannot be executed independently, this activity is not a use case of the information system. Furthermore, we have the use cases Issue information, Reserve lecture hall, and Create course, where Reserve lecture hall extends the use case Create course. Figure 3.19 shows the resulting use cases.

3. *Identifying associations*

Now we have to associate our actors and the use cases (see Fig. 3.20). Note that we now have two fewer actors than potential candidates identified (see Fig. 3.18). There are no longer any students—students may not use the information system in the form that we have modeled it. And there is no longer a notification system as this is considered to be part of the student office.

Finally, we need a meaningful description of the use cases.

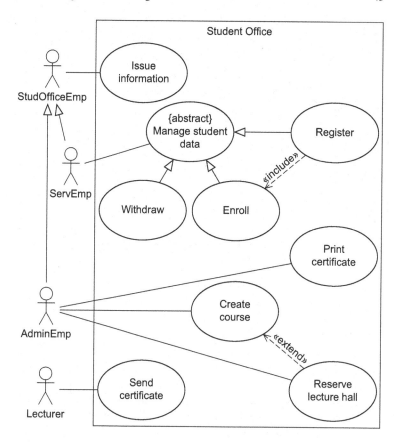

Figure 3.20
Use case diagram of the
information system of
the student office of a
university

4. *Describing the use cases*

Table 3.2 shows the description of the use case Print certificate as an
example.

Table 3.2
Use case description for
Print certificate

Name:	Print certificate
Short description:	On request from a student, an employee prints the student's certificate for a course on paper.
Precondition:	All data relevant for the certificate has been sent and the student has been graded.
Postcondition:	Certificate is available to the student in printed form.
Error situations:	Printer is not working.
System state in the event of an error:	Certificate is not printed.
Actors:	AdminEmp
Trigger:	Student requests printed certificate.
Standard process:	(1) Student enters the student office and requests a certificate. (2) AdminEmp enters the student's matriculation number. (3) AdminEmp selects the certificate. (4) AdminEmp enters the print command. (5) System confirms that the certificate was printed. (6) Certificate is handed over to the student.
Alternative processes:	(1') Student requests certificate via e-mail. (2-5) As above (6') Certificate is sent by post.

3.8 Summary

The use case diagram describes the behavior of a system from the view of the user. This means that this diagram presents the functionalities that the system offers but does not address the internal implementation details. The boundaries of the system—what can the system do and what can it not do?—are clearly defined. The users (actors) are always outside the system and use the functionalities of the system, which are depicted in the form of use cases. The relationship between a use case and an actor is referred to as an association. To keep use case diagrams as compact as possible, generalization is supported for both actors and use cases, which allows the extraction of common properties. Use cases can also access the functionality provided by other use cases by means of «include» and «extend» relationships. The most important notation elements are summarized in Table 3.3.

Name	Notation	Description
System		Boundaries between the system and the users of the system
Use case		Unit of functionality of the system
Actor	«actor» X or X	Role of the users of the system
Association	X — A	X participates in the execution of A
Generalization (use case)	A ◁ B	B inherits all properties and the entire behavior of A
Generalization (actor)	X ◁ Y	Y inherits from X; Y participates in all use cases in which X participates
Extend relationship	A «extend» B	B extends A: optional incorporation of use case B into use case A
Include relationship	A «include» B	A includes B: required incorporation of use case B into use case A

Table 3.3
Notation elements for the use case diagram

Chapter 4
The Class Diagram

We use the *class diagram* to model the static structure of a system, thus describing the elements of the system and the relationships between them. These elements and the relationships between them do not change over time. For example, students have a name and a matriculation number and attend various courses. This sentence covers a small part of the university structure and does not lose any validity even over years. It is only the specific students and courses that change.

Class diagram

The class diagram is without doubt the most widely used UML diagram. It is applied in various phases of the software development process. The level of detail or abstraction of the class diagram is different in each phase. In the early project phases, a class diagram allows you to create a conceptual view of the system and to define the vocabulary to be used. You can then refine this vocabulary into a programming language up to the point of implementation. In the context of object-oriented programming, the class diagram visualizes the classes a software system consists of and the relationships between these classes. Due to its simplicity and its popularity, the class diagram is ideally suited for quick sketches. However, you can also use it to generate program code automatically. In practice, the class diagram is also often used for documentation purposes.

Before we introduce the concepts of the class diagram, let us first take a look at *objects*, which are modeled in *object diagrams*. Object diagrams allow you to depict concrete objects that appear in a system at a specific point in time. Classes provide schemas for characterizing objects and objects are instances of classes. The object diagram visualizes instances of classes that are modeled in a class diagram.

Object diagram

© Springer International Publishing Switzerland 2015
M. Seidl et al., *UML @ Classroom*, Undergraduate Topics
in Computer Science, DOI 10.1007/978-3-319-12742-2_4

4.1 Objects

A system contains numerous different individuals. Individuals might be not only persons but also animals, plants, inanimate objects, artifacts, etc. that can be identified uniquely. For example, as part of her *IT Studies* program, *Helen Lewis* attends the lecture *Object-Oriented Modeling (OOM)* at the university. *Helen Lewis*, *IT Studies*, and *Object-Oriented Modeling* are individuals (concrete objects) in a university administration system and are in a relationship with one another.

Figure 4.1
Example of an object
diagram

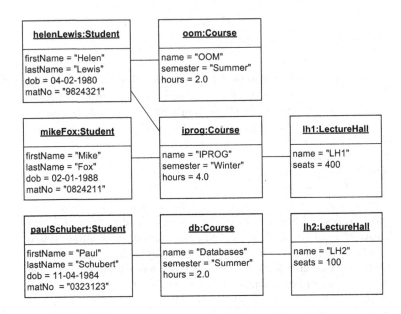

In UML, we depict concrete *objects* of a system and their relationships (*links*) using *object diagrams*. Figure 4.1 shows a small object diagram. It contains three student objects: helenLewis, mikeFox, and paulSchubert. The first name and the last name of the object helenLewis are *Helen* and *Lewis* respectively. We also know the date of birth and matriculation number for each of these objects. The system contains the three courses oom (Object-Oriented Modeling), iprog (Introduction to Programming), and db (Databases). The course iprog takes place in lecture hall lh1 and the course db takes place in lecture hall lh2. There is no corresponding information for oom. Student helenLewis attends the two courses oom and iprog. Student mikeFox also attends iprog; course db is attended only by student paulSchubert (at least, among these three students).

Object diagram

An object has a unique identity and a number of characteristics that describe it in more detail. It rarely appears in isolation in a system; instead, it usually interacts and communicates with other objects. The relationships between the objects are referred to as *links*. The characteristics of an object include its *structural characteristics* (attributes) and its *behavior* (in the form of operations). Whilst concrete values are assigned to the attributes in the object diagram, operations are generally not depicted. Operations are identical for all objects of a class and are therefore usually described exclusively for the class.

In the object diagram, an object is shown as a rectangle which can be subdivided into multiple compartments. The first compartment always contains information in the form objectName:Class. This information is centered and underlined. In Figure 4.1 for example, helenLewis and oom are object names and Student and Course are classes. The object name or the specification of the class may be omitted. If only a class name is given, it must be preceded by a colon. If the class name is omitted, the colon is also omitted. If the object name is omitted, this object is referred to as an *anonymous object*. Examples of different notation alternatives are shown in Figure 4.2.

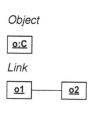

Object

Link

Anonymous object

| **maxMiller** | **maxMiller:Person** | **:Person** |

| **maxMiller** | **maxMiller:Person** | **:Person** |
| firstName = "Max"
lastName = "Miller"
dob = 03-05-1973 | firstName = "Max"
lastName = "Miller"
dob = 03-05-1973 | firstName = "Max"
lastName = "Miller"
dob = 03-05-1973 |

Figure 4.2
Notation alternatives for objects

If the rectangle has a second compartment, this compartment contains the attributes of the object and the current values of these attributes (see Fig. 4.1 and Fig. 4.2). A link is represented as a continuous line connecting the objects that are in a relationship with one another. Although the name of an object must be unique, different objects can have attributes with identical values. If, in our system, there were two people with the first name *Max* and the last name *Miller*, and both were born on the same day, we would have to represent them using different objects with different object names (e.g., maxMiller1 and maxMiller2). However, their attribute values would be identical.

The values of the attributes generally change over time. For example, if the person *Max Miller* changes his last name, the individual as a whole does not change, only the value of the attribute lastName. The object diagram therefore always represents only a snapshot of objects at a specific moment in time and the objects can develop further and change as time passes. If specific objects are not represented in the object diagram, this does not mean that they do not exist; it merely expresses that the unrecorded objects are not important for the moment.

From object to class

Many individuals that appear in a system have identical characteristics and behavior. For example, persons always have a first name, a last name, and a date of birth. Students also have a matriculation number. Courses always have a name and a number of hours, as well as a semester in which they take place. Information about the lecture halls includes the number of seats available. If every person, every course, and every lecture hall of the system were to be modeled individually, the model would soon become over-complicated and impossible to maintain. Using classes enables you to describe similar objects without having to detail each and every object individually.

4.2 Classes

Class

A *class* is the construction plan for a set of similar *objects* that appear in the system to be specified. Classes can characterize, for example, persons (e.g., students), things (e.g., buildings), events (e.g., courses or exams), or even abstract concepts such as groups. In object-oriented programming languages like Java [4], programs are created based on classes. Figure 4.3 compares a class definition from a UML class diagram with a class definition in Java.

Figure 4.3
Definition of a class in
UML and Java

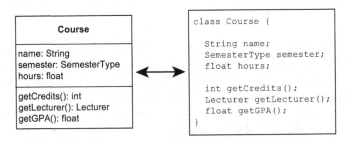

Instance
Characteristics of
classes ...

Objects represent the concrete forms of classes and are referred to as their *instances*. The relevant characteristics of the instances of a class are described through the definition of structural characteristics (*attributes*) and behavior (*operations*). Operations enable objects to communicate with one another and to act and react.

An attribute allows you to store information that is known for all instances but that generally has different specific values for each instance. Operations specify how specific behavior can be triggered on individual objects. For example, the class Course from Figure 4.3 has the attributes name and hours. Figure 4.1 shows concrete forms of these attributes. Possible operations of this class are getGPA() and getLecturer(), which return the grade point average or lecturer for a course respectively.

... are attributes and operations

To ensure that a model remains clear and understandable, we generally do not model all of the details of the content: we only include the information that is relevant for the moment and for the system to be implemented. This means that we *abstract* from reality to make the model less complex and to avoid an unnecessary flood of information. In the model, we restrict ourselves to the essentials. For example, in a university administration system, it is important to be able to manage the names and matriculation numbers of the students; in contrast, their shoe size is irrelevant and is therefore not included.

Level of detail

Abstraction

4.2.1 Notation

In a class diagram, a class is represented by a rectangle that can be subdivided into multiple compartments. The first compartment must contain the name of the class, which generally begins with a capital letter and is positioned centered in bold font (e.g., Course in Figure 4.4).

According to common naming conventions, class names are singular nouns. The class name should describe the class using vocabulary typical for the application domain. The second compartment of the rectangle contains the *attributes* of the class, and the third compartment the

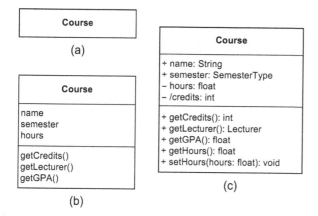

(a)

(b)

(c)

Figure 4.4
Representation of a class and its characteristics

operations of the class. The contents of these compartments are positioned left-justified and are optional. In general, the level of detail in
these compartments reflects the respective phase of the software development process in which the class is being examined. While the class
diagram excerpt in Figure 4.4(a) does not contain any details of the
class Course, the diagram in Figure 4.4(b) is the result of a more detailed analysis of the characteristic features of courses, showing specifically that the class Course contains three attributes and three operations. The diagram in Figure 4.4(c) presents even more detail (such as
the type information and visibilities), including information that is relevant for implementation or for automatic code generation. If specific
information is not included in the diagram, this does not mean that it
does not exist; it simply means that this information is not relevant at
this moment in time or is not included for practical reasons, for example, to prevent the diagram from becoming over-complicated. Attributes
and operations are usually accessed via their names, which, according
to naming conventions, begin with a lower case letter.

4.2.2 Attributes

Attribute   Figure 4.5 shows the syntax of attributes. An attribute has at least a
name. The type of the attribute may be specified after the name using : Type. Possible attribute types include primitive data types, such
Type   as integer and string, composite data types, for example a date, an enumeration, or user-defined classes (see Section 4.8). By specifying name:
String, for example, we define the attribute name with type String. Figure 4.6 shows further examples of attribute types. We will look at the
subsequent, optional multiplicity specification in more detail in the next
section.

Figure 4.5
Syntax of the attribute
specification

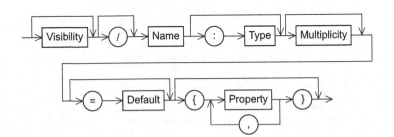

To define a *default value* for an attribute, you specify = *Default*, where *Default* is a user-defined value or expression (see Fig. 4.6). The system uses the default value if the value of the attribute is not set explicitly by the user. Thus it is impossible that at some point in time, an attribute has no value. For example, if in our system, a person must always have a password, a default password *pw123* is set when a new person is entered in the system. This password is valid until it is reseted.

Default value

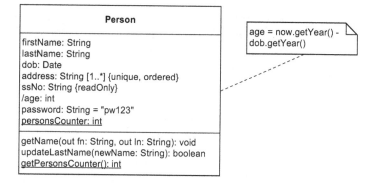

Figure 4.6
Properties of attributes

You can specify additional *properties* of the attribute within curly brackets. For example, the property {readOnly} means that the attribute value cannot be changed once it has been initialized. In the example in Figure 4.6, the social security number ssNo is an attribute that must not be changed. Further properties will be introduced in the next section within the description of multiplicity specifications.

Properties of attributes

The specification of a forward slash before an attribute name indicates that the value of this attribute is derived from other attributes. An example of a *derived attribute* is a person's age, which can be calculated from the date of birth. In Figure 4.6, a note contains a calculation rule for determining a person's age. Depending on the development tool used, such notes are formulated in natural language, in a programming language, or in pseudocode. The optional visibility marker (+, −, #, or ~) in front of an attribute name or operation name as shown in Figure 4.4(c) is discussed in detail on page 58.

4.2.3 Multiplicities

The *multiplicity* of an attribute indicates how many values an attribute can contain. This enables you to define arrays, just like in programming languages. The multiplicity is shown as an interval enclosed by square

Multiplicity

brackets in the form [minimum .. maximum], whereby minimum and maximum are natural numbers indicating the lower and upper limits of the
interval. The value of minimum must be smaller than or equal to the
value of maximum. If there is no upper limit for the interval, this is expressed with an asterisk *. The class Person in Figure 4.6 contains an
attribute address: String [1..*]. This denotes that a person has at least one
and possibly multiple addresses. If minimum and maximum are identical, you do not have to specify the minimum and the two dots. For
example, [5] means that an attribute adopts exactly *five* values. The expression [*] is equivalent to [0..*]. If you do not specify a multiplicity for
an attribute, the value *1* is assumed as default, which specifies a single-
valued attribute. The valid notation for multiplicities is summarized in
Figure 4.7.

Figure 4.7
Syntax of the multiplicity
specification

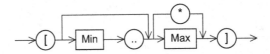

If an attribute can adopt multiple values, it makes sense to specify
whether the attribute is:

- A set (no fixed order of elements, no duplicates)
- A multi-set (no fixed order of elements, duplicates possible)
- An ordered set (fixed order, no duplicates)
- A list (fixed order, duplicates possible)

Unique, non-unique,
ordered, unordered   You can make this specification by combining the properties {non-
unique} and {unique}, which define whether duplicates are permitted or
not permitted, and {ordered} and {unordered}, which force or cancel a
fixed order of the attribute values. For example, the attribute address:
String [1..*] {unique, ordered} contains all the addresses for a person (see
Fig. 4.6). As each address should only be contained once, the attribute
is labeled {unique}. By specifying {ordered}, we express that the order
of the addresses is important. For example, the first address could be
interpreted as the main residence.

4.2.4 Operations

Operation   *Operations* are characterized by their name, their parameters, and the
type of their return value (see Fig. 4.8). When an operation is called in
a program, the behavior assigned to this operation is executed. In programming languages, an operation corresponds to a method declaration

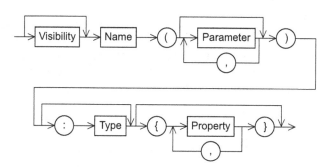

Figure 4.8
Syntax of the operation
specification

or function declaration which is defined but not implemented. The class
diagram is not suitable for describing the behavior of objects in detail
as it only models signatures of the operations that the objects provide;
it does not model how these operations are actually implemented. UML
offers special behavior diagrams for depicting the implementation of
operations, for example the activity diagram (see Chapter 7).

In a class diagram, the operation name is followed by a list of *pa-*   *Parameters*
rameters in parentheses. The list itself may be empty. A parameter is
depicted similarly to an attribute. The only obligatory information is the
name of the parameter. The addition of a type, a multiplicity, a default
value, and further properties, such as ordered, unique, or their negated
counterparts is optional (see Fig. 4.9).

The optional return value of an operation is specified with the type   *Return value*
of the return value. In Figure 4.6, the class Person has an operation
updateLastName(newName: String): boolean. The only parameter, new-
Name, has the type String and specifies the new name for a person. The
return value has the type boolean. If *true* is returned, the renaming was
successful, otherwise *false* is returned.

If required, you can also prepend a direction to the parameter name.   *Input and output*
This direction can have one of the following values: in, out, or inout (see   *parameters*
Fig. 4.9). The value indicates whether the parameter is an *input param-*
eter, an *output parameter*, or both. If a parameter has the direction in,
this indicates that when the operation is used, a value is expected from
this parameter. The specification of the direction out expresses that after
the execution of the operation, the parameter has adopted a new value.
If an operation should have multiple return values rather than just one,
you can express this using multiple parameters with the direction out.
The specification of inout indicates a combined input/output parameter.
If no direction is specified, in is the default value. In Figure 4.6, the operation getName(out fn: String, out ln: String) has two parameters with the
direction value out. For example, if we use the operation getName in a
program by calling getName(firstName, lastName), whereby

`firstName` and `lastName` are variables in the sense of an imperative programming language, successful execution of the operation produces the following results: the variable `firstName` contains the first name and the variable `lastName` contains the last name of the object of type Person on which the operation `getName` was called.

Figure 4.9
Syntax of the parameter
specification

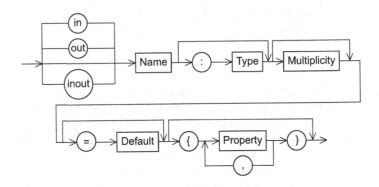

4.2.5 Visibility Markers

Visibility The *visibility* of attributes and operations specifies who is and who is not permitted to access them. If an attribute or operation does not have a visibility specified, no default visibility is assumed. Table 4.1 lists the types of visibilities and their meaning in UML. Only an object itself knows the values of attributes that are marked as private. In contrast, anyone can view attributes marked as public. Access to protected attributes is reserved for the class itself and its subclasses. If a class has a package attribute, only classes that are in the same package as this class may access this attribute. Accordingly, the visibility of an operation specifies who is permitted to use the functionality of the operation. Examples are given in Figure 4.4(c) on page 53. Note that the meaning of visibilities can vary in different programming and modeling languages even if they have the same name in the different languages.

Information hiding Visibilities are used to realize *information hiding*, an important concept in computing. Marking the attributes that represent the state of an object as private protects this state against unauthorized access. Access is therefore only possible via a clearly defined interface, such as via operations that are declared public.

In some cases, class diagrams contain only those attributes and operations that are visible externally. Attributes and operations of classes

that are marked as private are often omitted, as they are important for
the realization, that is, the implementation of a class, but not for its use.
Therefore, whether or not attributes and operations marked as private
are specified depends on the intention behind and the time of creation
of the class diagram.

Name	Symbol	Description
public	+	Access by objects of any classes permitted
private	−	Access only within the object itself permitted
protected	#	Access by objects of the same class and its subclasses permitted
package	~	Access by objects whose classes are in the same package permitted

Table 4.1
Visibilities

4.2.6 Class Variables and Class Operations

Attributes are usually defined at instance level. If, for example, a class
is realized in a programming language, memory is reserved for every attribute of an object when it is created. Such attributes are also referred to
as *instance variables* or *instance attributes*. In Figure 4.10 for example,
lastName and dob are instance variables. If, in an object-oriented program generated from this class of diagram, `person1` is an instance of
the class `Person`, for example, `person1.lastName` can be used to
refer to the last name of the person. Access to this person's date of birth
is not possible as the visibility of the attribute `dob` is private. To find
out the date of birth of `person1`, the function `person1.getDob()`
must be called. An operation such as getDob() can only be executed if
a corresponding instance that offers this operation was created beforehand. In our case, this is the instance `person1`. An operation may use
all visible instance variables.

Synonyms:

• *Instance variable*
• *Instance attribute*

In contrast to instance variables, *class variables* are created only
once for a class rather than separately for every instance of this class.
These variables are also referred to as *static attributes* or *class attributes*. Counters for the number of instances of a class (see Fig. 4.10)
or constants such as π are often realized as static attributes. In the
class diagram, static attributes are underlined, just like *static operations*.
Static operations, also called *class operations*, can be used if no instance
of the corresponding class was created. Examples of static operations
are mathematical functions such as `sin(x)` or constructors. Constructors are special functions called to create a new instance of a class. The
method invocation `Person.getPCounter()` uses the static opera-

Synonyms:

• *Class variable*
• *Class attribute*
• *Static attribute*

Synonyms:

• *Class operation*
• *Static operation*

tion `getPCounter()` defined in Figure 4.10; the operation is called
directly via the class and not via an instance. Unless stated otherwise,
attributes and operations denote instance attributes and instance operations in most object-oriented languages. We also follow this convention
in this book.

Figure 4.10
Translation of a class from
UML to Java

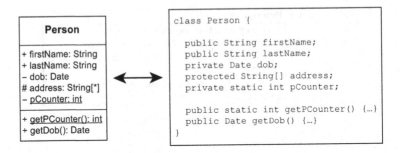

4.3 Associations

Association

Associations between classes model possible relationships, known as
links, between instances of the classes. They describe which classes are
potential communication partners. If their attributes and operations have
the corresponding visibilities, the communication partners can access
each other's attributes and operations. A class diagram can be viewed
as a graph in which the classes represent the nodes and the associations
represent the edges. Figure 4.11 depicts a class diagram and a valid
object diagram. The class diagram shows that the classes Professor and
Student are related via the association givesLectureFor. In the role as a
lecturer, a professor has zero or more students and one student has zero
or more professors in the role of lecturer. The object diagram models a
concrete scenario.

4.3.1 Binary Associations

Binary association

Reading direction

A *binary association* allows us to associate the instances of two classes
with one another. The relationships are shown as edges (solid line) between the partner classes involved. The edge can be labeled with the
name of the association optionally followed by the *reading direction*, a
small, black triangle. The reading direction is directed towards one end

Figure 4.11
Example of a binary asso-
ciation in a class diagram
and a valid object diagram

of the association and merely indicates in which direction the reader of
the diagram should "read" the association name. We have already seen
a binary association with reading direction in Figure 4.11. In this diagram, the reading direction indicates that professors give lectures for
students and not the other way around.

If the edge is directed, that is, at least one of the two ends has an open
arrowhead, navigation from an object to its partner object is possible. In
simple terms, *navigability* indicates that an object knows its partner objects and can therefore access their visible attributes and operations. The
navigation direction has nothing to do with the reading direction, as the
example in Figure 4.11 shows. The reading direction indicates that professors give lectures for students. However, the navigability specified
indicates that students can access the visible characteristics of professors whose lectures they attend. In contrast, a professor cannot access
the visible characteristics of the students who attend the professor's lecture because the professor does not know them.

Navigability

A non-navigable association end is indicated by the explicit specification of an X at the association end concerned. For example, if such
an X appears at the association end of A for an association between the
classes A and B, this means that B cannot access the attributes and operations of A—not even the public ones. Bidirectional edges without
arrowheads or X at their ends do not provide any information about the
navigation direction but in practice, bidirectional navigability is usually
assumed. The navigation direction represents a hint for the subsequent
implementation because in object-oriented programming languages, associations are realized as references to the associated objects. An association can also be represented in this way in the class diagram, that is, as
an attribute with the appropriate multiplicity, whereby the type of the attribute is the class of the corresponding partner objects. This representation has the same semantics as a navigable association end. Figure 4.12

Non-navigability

Figure 4.12
Associations in UML and
Java

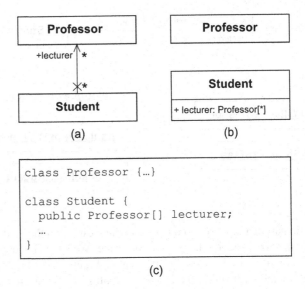

(a)   (b)

```
class Professor {…}

class Student {
    public Professor[] lecturer;
    …
}
```

(c)

shows (a) a class diagram in which the student-professor relationship is
modeled explicitly as an association, (b) a class diagram in which the
relationship is represented by an attribute in the class Student, and (c)
the translation into Java. The class diagram in Figure 4.12(a) is prefer-
able, as here the relationship between the classes is visualized explicitly
and it is visible immediately, while in the alternative in Figure 4.12(b),
the association between Student and Professor can only be recognized
by reading the type information of the attribute lecturer.

Figure 4.13
Examples of multiplicity
specifications in binary
associations

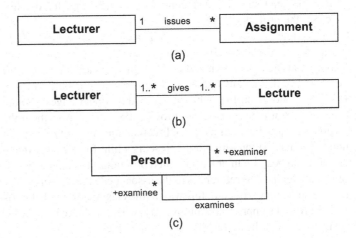

In the same way that multiplicities of attributes and parameters are specified, *multiplicities* of associations are given as an interval in the form minimum..maximum. They specify the number of objects that may be associated with exactly one object of the opposite side. The values that the minimum and maximum may adopt are natural numbers and an asterisk ∗, which expresses that there is no restriction. If minimum and maximum are identical, one value and the dots can be omitted. Again, 0..∗ means the same as ∗. Figure 4.13 shows examples of multiplicity specifications for binary associations. Figure 4.13(a) shows that a lecturer may issue no, one, or multiple assignments and that an assignment is issued by exactly one lecturer. No assignment may exist without an association to a lecturer. Figure 4.13(b) shows that a lecturer gives at least one lecture and a lecture is given by at least one lecturer. Finally, Figure 4.13(c) shows that a person in the role of examiner can examine any number (≥ 0) of persons and a person in the role of examinee can be examined by any number of examiners. In the example in Figure 4.13(c), the model does not exclude the case that persons may examine themselves. If this should be prohibited, additional constraints must be specified.

Multiplicity

You may also label the association ends with role names. A *role* describes the way in which an object is involved in an association relationship, that is, what role it plays in the relationship. In the association in Figure 4.13(c), the Person adopts the role of examiner or examinee.

Role

To express that an object of class A is to be associated with an object of class B or an object of class C but not with both, you can specify an *xor constraint* (exclusive or). To indicate that two associations from the same class are mutually exclusive, they can be connected by a dashed line labeled {xor}. For example, an exam can take place either in an office or in a lecture hall but not in both (see Fig. 4.14).

xor constraint

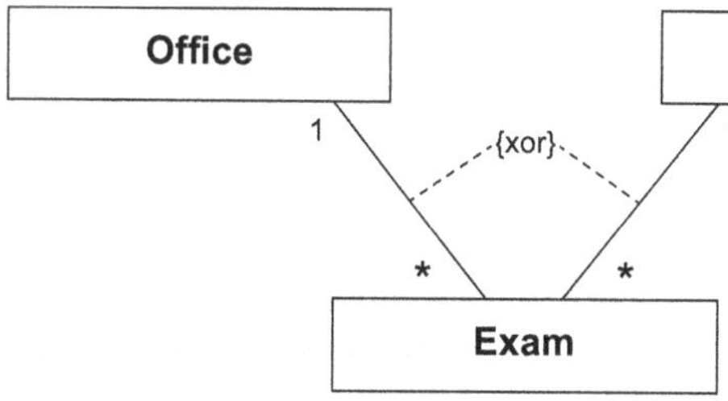

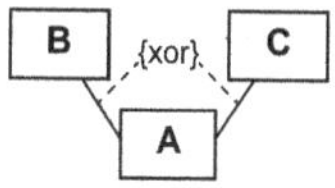

Figure 4.14
Examples of associations with xor constraints

4.3.2 N-Ary Associations

N-ary association

Multiplicities for n-ary associations

If more than two partner objects are involved in a relationship, you can model this using an *n-ary association*. An n-ary association is represented with a hollow diamond in the center. The diamond is connected with all partners of the relationship by means of an undirected edge. The name of the association is specified next to the diamond. There are no navigation directions for n-ary associations; however, multiplicities and role names are possible. Multiplicities define how many objects of a role/class may be assigned to a fixed $(n-1)$-tuple of objects of the other roles/classes.

Figure 4.15 models the relationship grades between the instances of the classes Lecturer, Student, and Exam. The multiplicities are defined as follows: one specific student takes one specific exam with no lecturer (i.e., does not take this exam at all) or with precisely one lecturer. This explains the multiplicity 0..1 for the class Lecturer. One specific exam with one specific lecturer can of course be taken by any number of students and one specific student can be graded by one specific lecturer for any number of exams. In both cases, this is expressed by the multiplicity *. In this model, it is not possible that two or more lecturers grade one student for the same exam.

Figure 4.15
Example of n-ary (here ternary) association ...

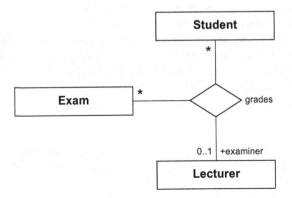

If you tried to express this ternary association with two binary associations, you would have a model with a different meaning. In the representation shown in Figure 4.16, an exam can be graded by multiple lecturers. The ternary association in Figure 4.15 clearly shows which lecturer a student passed a specific exam with—this is not the case with the diagram shown in Figure 4.16.

For example, with the model shown in Figure 4.15, it is possible to express that student s1 took the exam e1 with lecturer l1 and that student

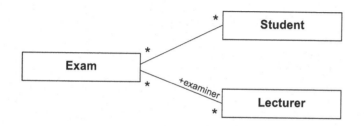

Figure 4.16
... versus example with two
binary associations ...

s2 took the same exam e1 with lecturer l2. With the model shown in
Figure 4.16, it is only possible to express that the students s1 and s2
took the exam e1 and that exam e1 has two examiners l1 and l2. With
this model, you cannot express which lecturer grades which student.

   As an alternative to the ternary association in Figure 4.15, an additional class can be introduced which is connected to the original classes
via binary associations (see Fig. 4.17). However, in this model it is possible that one student is graded multiple times for one and the same
exam what is not possible with the model of Figure 4.15.

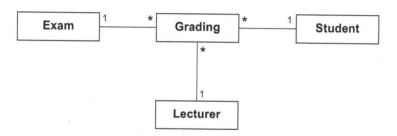

Figure 4.17
... versus example with
additional class

4.4 Association Classes

If you want to assign attributes or operations to the relationship between
one or more classes rather than to a class itself, you can do this using
an *association class*. An association class is represented by a class and
an association that are connected by a dashed line. The association can
be binary or n-ary. Although the representation includes multiple components, an association class is *one* language construct that has both the
properties of a class and the properties of an association. Therefore, in
a diagram, the class and association of an association class must have
the same name, although you do not have to name both (see the association classes Enrollment and Grade in Fig. 4.18). An association class

Association class

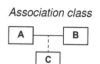

Figure 4.18
Examples of association
classes

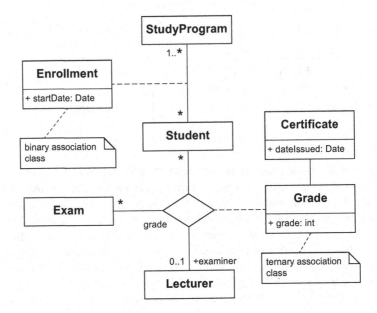

can also have associations with other classes. In Figure 4.18, the association class Grade, which contains information about a student's grade for a specific exam, is associated with the class Certificate.

In general, you cannot replace an association class with a "normal" class which is itself associated with the original two associated classes, as shown by the following example. Let us assume that we want to model that a student enrolls for at least one study program and has precisely one enrollment for each chosen study program. In turn, any number (≥ 0) of students can enroll for one specific study program. This situation is shown in Figure 4.19(a).

Figure 4.19(b) shows the attempt to model this situation with only "normal" classes. An enrollment is assigned to precisely one student

Figure 4.19
Attempt to model an as-
sociation class with a
"normal" class and cor-
responding relationships

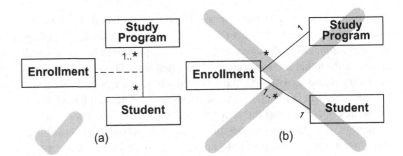

and precisely one study program, while one study program is related to any number of enrollment objects. A student has at least one enrollment. So far the requirements are met. However, if we examine the diagram more closely, we see that in Figure 4.19(b), a student can have multiple enrollments for one and the same study program, which is not the intention. In contrast, in Figure 4.19(a), a student can enroll for a specific study program only once.

If duplicates are explicitly required for an association class, at least one association end must be identified as {non-unique}. If this property is not specified explicitly, the default value {unique} is assumed. In Figure 4.20(a), a student can only be granted an exam meeting to discuss the result of the student's written exam once. Figure 4.20(b) shows a more student-friendly model. There, the use of {non-unique} allows a student to have more than one exam meeting.

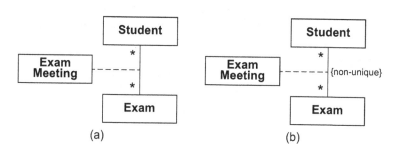

Figure 4.20
Example of {unique} and {non-unique} association ends

4.5 Aggregations

An aggregation is a special form of association that is used to express that instances of one class are parts of an instance of another class. UML differentiates between two types: *shared aggregation* and *composition*. Both are represented by a diamond at the association end of the class that stands for the "whole". The differentiation between composition and shared aggregation is indicated by a solid diamond for a composition and a hollow diamond for a shared aggregation. Both are transitive and asymmetric associations. In this case, transitivity means that if B is part of A and C is part of B, C is also part of A. Asymmetry expresses that it is not possible for A to be part of B and B to be part of A simultaneously.

Aggregation

Parts-whole relationship

Figure 4.21
Examples of shared
aggregations

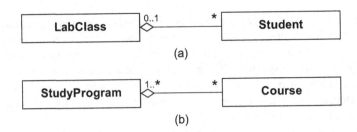

(a)

(b)

4.5.1 Shared Aggregations

Shared aggregation

In the UML standard, a *shared aggregation* has intentionally informal semantics. In principle, a shared aggregation expresses a weak belonging of the parts to a whole, meaning that parts also exist independently of the whole. The multiplicity at the aggregating end may be greater than 1, meaning that an element can be part of multiple other elements simultaneously. Shared aggregations can therefore span a directed acyclic graph. Figure 4.21 shows two examples of the use of a shared aggregation. In Figure 4.21(a), a lab class consists of any number of students. However, a student can participate in a maximum of one lab class. In Figure 4.21(b), a study program is made up of any (≥ 0) number of courses. A course is assigned to at least one (≥ 1) study program.

4.5.2 Compositions

Composition

The use of a *composition* expresses that a specific part can only be contained in at most one composite object at one specific point in time. This results in a maximum multiplicity of 1 at the aggregating end. The composite objects therefore form a forest of trees, indicating an existence dependency between the composite object and its parts; if the composite object is deleted, its parts are also deleted. Figure 4.22 shows examples of compositions. A lecture hall is part of a building. Due to the multiplicity 1, there is an existence dependency between elements of these two classes. The lecture hall cannot exist without the building. If the building no longer exists, the lecture hall also does not exist anymore. The situation is different for a beamer which is also associated with a lecture hall by a composition. However, the multiplicity 0..1 is specified at the aggregating end. This means that the beamer can exist without the lecture hall, that is, it can be removed from the lecture hall. If the beamer is located in the lecture hall and the lecture hall ceases

Figure 4.22
Examples of compositions

to exist—for example, because the building is torn down—the beamer also ceases to exist. However, if it was removed from the lecture hall beforehand, it continues to exist.

A shared aggregation is differentiated from an association only by the fact that it explicitly visualizes a "part of" relationship. In a composition, the existence dependency signifies a far stronger bond between the composite object and its parts, which means that a composition and an association are not interchangeable. A composition is usually used if the parts are physically embedded in the composite object or are only visible for the composite object. If the parts are referenced externally, this can indicate that a shared aggregation is sufficient. Furthermore, if the composite object is deleted or copied, its parts are also deleted or copied when a composition is used.

Existence dependency of a composite object's parts

4.6 Generalizations

Different classes often have common characteristics. For example, in Figure 4.23, the classes Student, ResearchAssociate, and AdministrativeEmployee all have the attributes name, address, dob, and ssNo. Students and employees of both types are distinguished by further characteristics specific to the respective class: a student has a matriculation

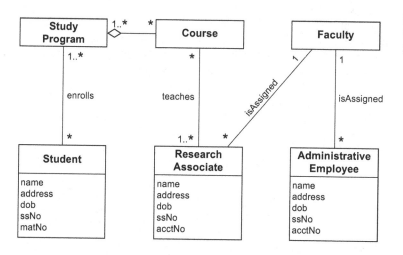

Figure 4.23
Class diagram without generalization

number and has enrolled for at least one study program; employees have a checking account and are assigned to a faculty. Instances of the class ResearchAssociate are in a teaches relationship with any number of instances of the class Course.

We can use a generalization relationship to highlight commonalities between classes, meaning that we no longer have to define these common characteristics multiple times. Conversely, we can use the generalization to derive more specific classes from existing classes. If we want to add a class Professor, which is a subclass of ResearchAssociate, in Figure 4.23, we use the generalization to avoid having to copy the characteristics of the class ResearchAssociate to the class Professor.

4.6.1 Inheritance

Inheritance from superclass to subclass

Synonyms:

- *Inheritance*
- *Generalization*
- *"Is a" relationship*

The *generalization relationship* expresses that the characteristics (attributes and operations) and associations that are specified for a general class (*superclass*) are passed on to its *subclasses*. Therefore, the generalization relationship is also referred to as *inheritance*. This means that every instance of a subclass is simultaneously an indirect instance of the superclass. The subclass "possesses" all instance attributes and class attributes and all instance operations and class operations of the superclass provided these have not been marked with the visibility private. The subclass may also have further attributes and operations or enter into other relationships independently of its superclass. Accordingly, operations that originate from the subclass or the superclass can be executed directly on the instance of a subclass.

Generalization notation

A generalization relationship is represented by an arrow with a hollow, triangular arrowhead from the subclass to the superclass, for example from Student to Person in Fig. 4.24. The name of a superclass must be selected such that it represents an umbrella term for the names of its subclasses. To ensure that there are no direct instances of the class Person, we label this class with the keyword {abstract}. The class Person therefore becomes an *abstract class* and only its non-abstract subclasses can be instantiated. We will look at details of abstract classes in Section 4.7 on page 72.

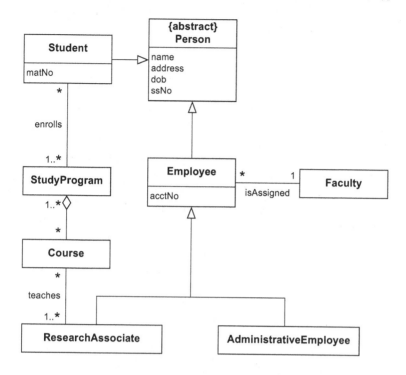

Figure 4.24
Class diagram with
generalization

The generalization relationship is also referred to as an "is a" relationship. For example, every student is a person (see Fig. 4.24). Every research associate and every administrative employee is an employee and, due to the transitivity of the generalization relationship, every administrative employee is also a person. If, as in object-oriented programming languages, we consider a class to be a type, subclasses and superclasses are equivalent to subtypes and supertypes.

Transitivity of the generalization relationship

Subtype and supertype equivalent to subclass and superclass

UML allows *multiple inheritance*, meaning that a class may have multiple superclasses. For example, a tutor is both an employee of the university and a student (see Fig. 4.25). Due to the transitivity of inheritance, single inheritance creates an inheritance hierarchy, whereas multiple inheritance creates a (directed acyclic) inheritance graph.

Multiple inheritance

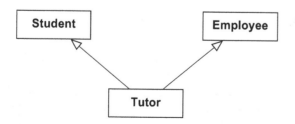

Figure 4.25
Example of multiple
inheritance

4.6.2 Classification

Classification refers to the "instanceOf" relationship between an object and its class. In many object-oriented programming languages, an object can usually only be the direct instance of precisely one class.

Multiple classification

In contrast, UML allows *multiple classification*. With multiple classification, an object can be an instance of multiple classes without these classes having to be associated with one another in an inheritance relationship. In contrast to multiple inheritance, no new class inheriting the characteristics of the superclasses involved is introduced.

For example, instances of Employee can be differentiated according to their job, that is, whether they are researchers or administrators, and whether they are financed directly via the university or via a project. Multiple classification means that an object can be an instance of multiple classes whose characteristics the object then has. In Figure 4.26, we have divided the generalization relationships into two groups. The

Generalization set

sets Job and Financing form *generalization sets* which group subclasses according to multiple independent criteria. Generalization sets can be described more precisely by the following constraints:

- *Overlapping* or *disjoint*: in an overlapping generalization set, an object may be an instance of multiple subclasses simultaneously. In a disjoint generalization set, an object may be an instance of a maximum of one subclass.
- *Complete* or *incomplete*: in a complete generalization set, each instance of the superclass must be an instance of at least one of the subclasses. In incomplete generalization sets, this is not necessary.

This results in four combinations: {complete, overlapping}, {incomplete, overlapping}, {complete, disjoint}, and {incomplete, disjoint}. If none of these constraints are specified explicitly, {incomplete, disjoint} is the default value. Examples are shown in Figure 4.26: an employee must belong to either the research or administrative personnel but not both. The employee can be financed directly via the university, via a project, via both, or in another, unspecified way, for example via a scholarship.

4.7 Abstract Classes vs. Interfaces

Abstract class

Classes that cannot be instantiated themselves are modeled as *abstract classes*. These are classes for which there are no objects—only their subclasses can be instantiated. Abstract classes are used exclusively to highlight common characteristics of their subclasses and are therefore

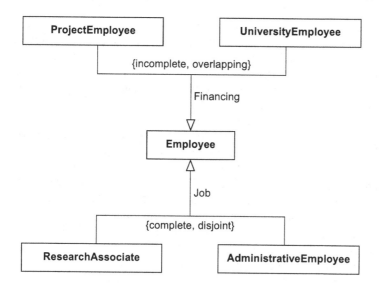

Figure 4.26
Example of multiple classification

only useful in the context of generalization relationships. Operations of abstract classes can also be labeled as abstract. An *abstract operation* does not offer any implementation itself. However, it requires an implementation in the concrete subclasses. Operations that are not abstract pass on their behavior to all subclasses.

Abstract operation

Abstract classes and abstract operations are either written in italic font or indicated by the specification of the keyword {abstract} before their name (see Fig. 4.27). In manually produced class diagrams in particular, the use of the second notation alternative is recommended, as italic handwriting is difficult to recognize.

Figure 4.27
Notation for abstract classes

In the example in Figure 4.28, the class Person is abstract. Hence, there cannot be any instances of Person itself but there can be instances of the specific subclasses Employee and Student.

Similarly to the abstract class, an *interface* also does not have an implementation or any direct instances. An interface represents a contract. The classes that enter into this contract, that is, the classes that implement the interface, obligate themselves to provide the behavior specified by the interface. In contrast to the relationship between an abstract class and its subclasses, an "is a" relationship between an interface and the classes that implement it is not necessary. Operations of interfaces never have an implementation.

Interface

An interface is denoted like a class but with the additional keyword
«interface» before the name. A dashed inheritance arrow with a hollow,
triangular arrowhead from a class to an interface signifies that this class
implements the interface. A dashed arrow with an open head with the
keyword «use» expresses that a class uses an interface. Let us look at
the example from Figure 4.28. The classes Person and Course implement the interface Printable. The classes that implement Printable must
provide an operation print(). This operation is different for every class.
For a course, the name and the number of hours are printed; for a Person, the name and address are printed. In the class Student, the operation
print() is specified again. This expresses that the Student extends the behavior of the operation print() inherited from Person. The method print()
is overwritten, meaning that the matriculation number is also printed.
For Employee this is not necessary, assuming that the behavior specified
for print() in Person is sufficient. The class Printer can now process each
class that implements the interface Printable. Thus, a specific print() can
be realized for each class and the class Printer remains unchanged.

Figure 4.28
Example of an interface

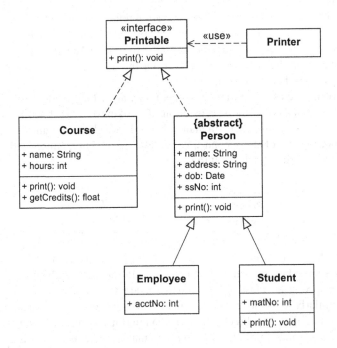

4.8 Data Types

Attributes, parameters, and return values of operations have a type that specifies which concrete forms they may take. For example, the name of a person has the type String. A type can be either a class or a *data type*. Instances of data types are also referred to as their *values*. In contrast to instances of classes (objects), values do not have their own identity. If two values are identical, they cannot be differentiated. For example, let us look at the class Book, whose instances are different copies of the book *UML@Classroom*. These copies can be uniquely identified and differentiated even though their attributes have the same content. However, different occurrences of a value, for example the number 2, cannot be differentiated. This differentiation becomes evident in the application of the comparison operation ==, as provided by Java for example. If we compare two variables of the type int (integer data type) and both variables have the same value, the result of the comparison operation is true. If we compare two different objects with ==, the result is false in general even if all attributes have the same values.

Class vs. data type

In UML, a data type is visualized in the same way as a class, with the difference that the name of the data type is annotated with the additional keyword «datatype» (see Fig. 4.29(b)). As the example in Figure 4.29(b) shows, data types can have an internal structure in the form of attributes. In UML, there are also two special forms of data types, namely primitive data types and enumerations.

Data type

Primitive data types do not have any internal structure. In UML there are four pre-defined primitive data types: Boolean, Integer, UnlimitedNatural, and String. User-defined primitive data types are identified by the specification of the keyword «primitive». Primitive data types may have operations (see Fig. 4.29(a)) that are executed on their values.

Primitive data type

Enumerations are data types whose values are defined in a list. The notation is the same as for a class with the specific identification «enumeration». In Figure 4.29(c), the enumeration AcademicDegree is defined. This enumeration lists all academic degrees that are known in our system. Therefore, attributes of the type AcademicDegree may take the values bachelor, master, and phd. These values are called *literals*.

Enumeration

Literal

«primitive» **Float**	«datatype» **Date**	«enumeration» **AcademicDegree**
round(): void	day month year	bachelor master phd
(a)	(b)	(c)

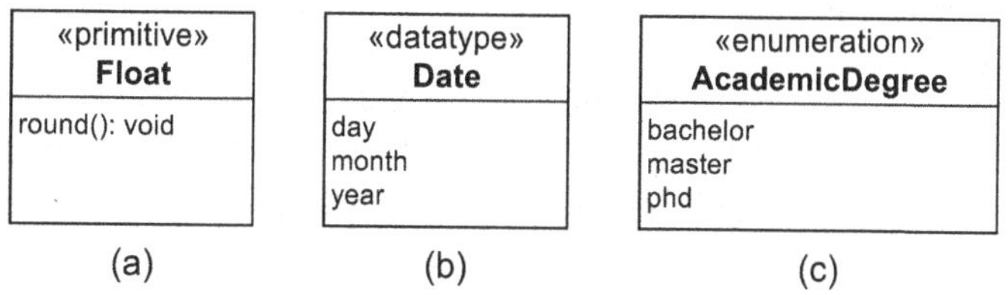

Figure 4.29
Examples of data types

User-defined types are used as specified in the syntax description of attributes and operations in Figure 4.5 (page 54) and in Figure 4.8 (page 57). Let us look at the type definitions from Figure 4.29 again. These could be used in the following attribute definitions: weight: Float, dob: Date, and title: AcademicDegree [*].

4.9 Creating a Class Diagram

UML describes the syntax and semantics of classes and their relationships but not how the classes and relationships are constructed. Unfortunately, it is not possible in principle to completely extract classes and their characteristics from a natural language text automatically. However, there are guidelines for creating a class diagram. Nouns such as person, employee, course, etc. often indicate classes. In contrast, names of values such as *Paul* or *object-oriented modeling* and expressions that indicate the relationships between potential classes are rarely classes. Values of attributes are often expressed by adjectives or also by nouns and operations often result from verbs. The following three aspects are important: which operations can an object of a class execute? Which events, to which the object must be able to react, can theoretically occur? And finally, which other events occur as a result? If the values of an attribute can be derived from another attribute, for example, if the age of a person can be calculated from their date of birth, it should be identified as a derived attribute. Further, it is essential to consider not only the current requirements but also the extensibility of the system.

As we now know how to derive a class diagram from a textual specification, we will do so for the following requirement specification:

Information system of a
university
- A university consists of multiple faculties which are composed of various institutes. Each faculty and each institute has a name. An address is known for each institute.
- Each faculty is led by a dean, who is an employee of the university.
- The total number of employees is known. Employees have a social security number, a name, and an e-mail address. There is a distinction between research and administrative personnel.
- Research associates are assigned to at least one institute. The field of study of each research associate is known. Furthermore, research associates can be involved in projects for a certain number of hours, and the name, starting date, and end date of the projects are known. Some research associates teach courses. They are called lecturers.
- Courses have a unique number (ID), a name, and a weekly duration in hours.

1. *Identifying the classes*

First, we must identify the elements that occur in the system University that identify the classes. These are shown in Figure 4.30.

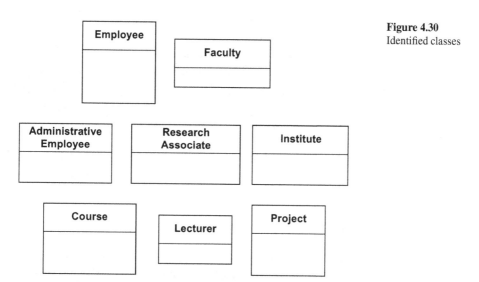

Figure 4.30
Identified classes

As we can see, University is not a separate class. We have not forgotten it—we have intentionally not included it. We are using the class diagram to describe the system University, hence the instance of our model contains those objects that occur within a university, for example, the Vienna University of Technology. If we included a class University which itself consists of other classes from Figure 4.30, we could model multiple university information systems simultaneously. Our model would then also describe, for example, the Johannes Kepler University Linz.

2. *Identifying the attributes*

We can now describe our classes in more detail using attributes. The classes and their attributes are shown in Figure 4.31.
We have defined meaningful data types for our attributes even though these are not included in the specification. We also set the visibility of all attributes to public so that in this phase, we do not have to think about which attributes are visible from the outside and which are not. The attribute counter of the class Employee is defined as a class attribute as its values do not belong to an instance. This attribute is increased when an instance of the class Employee is created.

Figure 4.31
Classes and their attributes

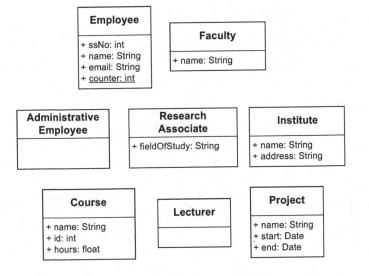

3. *Identifying the relationships between classes*

Classes can be linked with one another in three ways. They can be in a sub-/superclass relationship (generalization), be related by means of an aggregation, or linked via associations.

4.9.1 Generalizations

The following sentences strongly indicate a generalization relationship: "There is a distinction between research and administrative personnel." and "Some research associates teach courses. Then they are called lecturers." We model these generalization relationships as shown in Figure 4.32. As every employee of a university belongs to either the research or administrative personnel, we can set the class Employee to abstract.

4.9.2 Associations and Aggregations

To complete the class diagram, we need to add the associations and aggregations and their corresponding multiplicities. The classes Lecturer and Course are linked by means of the association teaches. An employee leads the faculty. Here the employee takes the role of a dean. A faculty

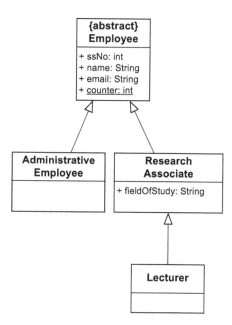

Figure 4.32
Identified generalization
relationships

consists of multiple institutes. We assume that there is an existence dependency which we model with a composition. Research associates are assigned to an institute, meaning they are part of an institute. Using a composition here would be incorrect as there is no existence dependency between instances of Employee and Institute. However, a shared aggregation is possible in order to represent the parts-whole relationship explicitly. Finally, we have the involvement of research associates in projects, whereby we know the number of hours of participation. For this we need the association class Participation. This association class further details the relationship between the project and the research associate with the number of hours. Figure 4.33 shows the complete class diagram for the given task.

Note that the resulting model is not unique even for such small examples; it depends on the one hand on the intended application, and on the other hand on the style of the modeler. For example, if we had created the model with the intention of generating code from it, we would perhaps have designed the interfaces more carefully and specified more differentiated visibilities. It is a matter of taste that Lecturer is a separate class but dean is a role. We could also have specified Lecturer as a role at the end of the association teaches which would have been defined between the classes ResearchAssociate and Course.

Figure 4.33
Class diagram of the in-
formation system of a
university

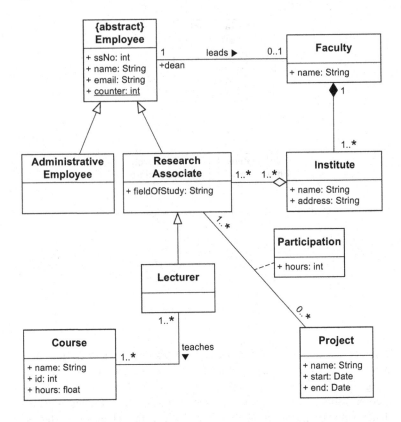

4.10 Code Generation

Forward engineering

Class diagrams are often created with the intention of implementing
the modeled elements in an object-oriented programming language. As
many of the concepts of the class diagram are available in identical or
similar form in object-oriented programming languages such as Java,
C#, or C++, in many cases a translation can take place automatically
and requires only minimal manual intervention. The class diagram is

Reverse engineering

also suitable for documenting existing program code, with the advan-
tage that the relationships between classes are represented graphically.
There are a number of tools for reverse engineering program code into
class diagrams automatically.

Data modeling also involves similar concepts to those of the class
diagram. For example, here the entity-relationship diagram (ER diagram) [14] is used—with the exception of different notation, it is very
similar to the class diagram. Both diagrams show the elements (classes
or entities) of a system and the relationships (associations or relations)

between them. In both cases, these elements are characterized by their attributes. Considerable differences are visible if we compare the focus of the two types of diagrams. While the ER diagram describes the elements of a database, the class diagram shows how to implement the modeled system in an object-oriented programming language. Thus, in the ER diagram, we can define key attributes that are required to identify entries in a table. This is not possible directly in a class diagram but it is also not necessary, as each object is identified by a unique object ID. In contrast, the specification of behavior, which is possible in the class diagram through operations, is not supported in the ER diagram. Therefore, the recommendation is to use the diagram type that is best for the problem in question. The following example again illustrates the connection between a class diagram (see Fig. 4.34) and the Java code generated from it (see Fig. 4.35).

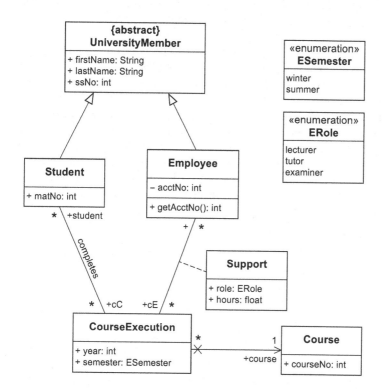

Figure 4.34
Class diagram from which code is to be generated

Many elements can be translated 1:1. Both abstract and concrete classes are adopted directly in the code with their attributes and operations. In the code, associations are represented as attributes. Note that the multiplicity of an association end is reflected in the type of the attribute. If the multiplicity is greater than one, we can use, for example, an array, as we did for the courses. Instead of arrays we could also use generic data types, for example the Java data type Collection; in contrast to arrays, with generic data types we do not have to know the size at initialization [4].

We have to make sure that we implement the navigation directions correctly. The navigation information provided in terms of arrowheads at the association ends tells us which class has to know about which other class—and this is realized via the attributes that model the association ends.

Some concepts, such as association classes or n-ary associations, do not exist directly in common programming languages such as Java. We thus have to consider how to simulate these concepts. Our example contains the association class Support. In the code this is implemented as a hash table. A hash table is a data structure that contains elements in the form (key, data). If the key (which must be unique) is known, the related data can be found efficiently.

Up to this point we have been able to describe the structure of elements and their relationships. We were not able to express behavior. In the above example we had only one operation, getAcctNo(), which returns the account number of the employee. The content of the method body was generated automatically as it is a getter method that encapsulates the access to a variable of the same name. For other operations, for example, operations that were intended to calculate something, the implementation cannot be derived automatically. UML offers other diagrams for modeling behavior and we will introduce these in the following chapters. To complete this chapter, Table 4.2 summarizes the most important concepts of the class and object diagrams.

Figure 4.35
Java code that can be gen-
erated automatically from
Fig. 4.34

```java
abstract class UniversityMember {
        public String firstName;
        public String lastName;
        public int ssNo;
}


class Student extends UniversityMember {
        public int matNo;
        public CourseExecution [] cC; // completed c.
}


class Employee extends UniversityMember {
        private int acctNo;
        public CourseExecution [] cE; // supported c.
        public int getAcctNo { return acctNo; }
}
class CourseExecution {
        public int year;
        public ESemester semester;
        public Student [] student;
        public Course course;
        public Hashtable support;
                // Key: employee
                // Value: (role, hours)
}


class Course {
        public int courseNo;
}


Enumeration ESemester {
        winter;
        summer;
}


Enumeration ERole {
        lecturer;
        tutor;
        examiner;
}
```

Table 4.2
Notation elements of the
class and object diagrams

Name	Notation	Description
Class	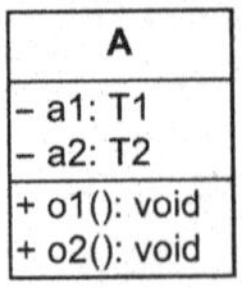 **A** – a1: T1 – a2: T2 + o1(): void + o2(): void	Description of the structure and behavior of a set of objects
Abstract class	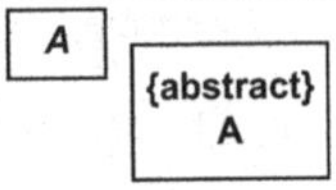 **A** / {abstract} **A**	Class that cannot be instantiated
Association	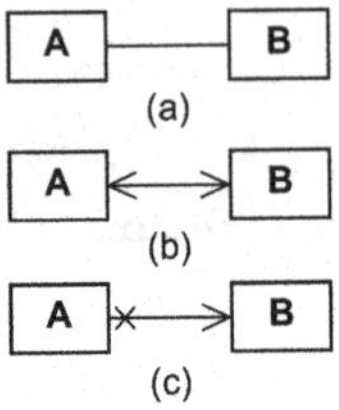 A — B (a) A ←→ B (b) A ⇥→ B (c)	Relationship between classes: navigability unspecified (a), navigable in both directions (b), not navigable in one direction (c)
N-ary association	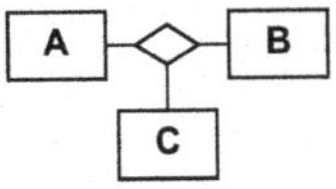 A ◇ B / C	Relationship between N (in this case 3) classes
Association class	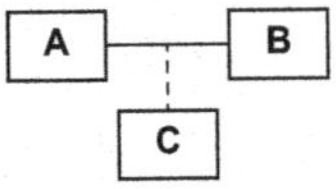 A ⋯ B / C	More detailed description of an association
xor relationship	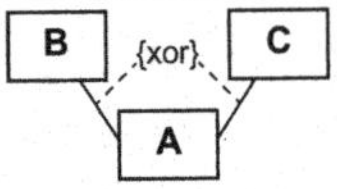 B {xor} C / A	An object of A is in a relationship with an object of B or with an object of C but not with both
Strong aggregation = composition	 A ◆— B	Existence-dependent parts-whole relationship (A is part of B; if B is deleted, related instances of A are also deleted)
Shared aggregation	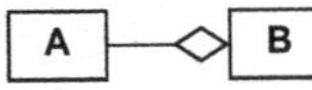 A —◇ B	Parts-whole relationship (A is part of B; if B is deleted, related instances of A need not be deleted)
Generalization	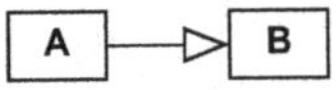 A —▷ B	Inheritance relationship (A inherits from B)
Object	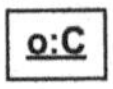 <u>o:C</u>	Instance of a class
Link	 <u>o1</u> — <u>o2</u>	Relationship between objects

Chapter 5
The State Machine Diagram

Over the course of its life, every system, or to be more precise every object, goes through a finite number of different states. Using a *state machine diagram*, you can model the possible states for the system or object in question, how state transitions occur as a consequence of occurring events, and what behavior the system or object exhibits in each state.

State machine diagram

As a simple example consider a lecture hall that can be in one of two states: free or occupied. When a lecture starts in the lecture hall, the state of the lecture hall changes from free to occupied. Once the respective event in the lecture hall has finished and the hall has been released again, its state reverts to free (see Fig. 5.1).

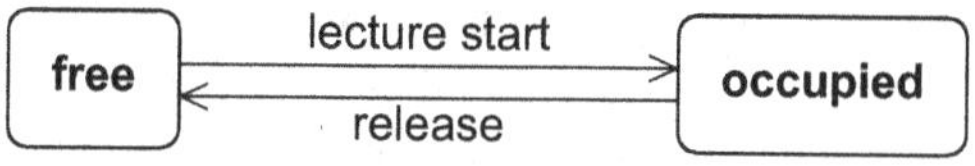

Figure 5.1
State machine diagram of a lecture hall (simplified presentation)

The state machine diagram is based on the work of David Harel [22] and uses concepts of finite automata. UML differentiates between two types of state machines, namely behavior state machines and protocol state machines. In this book, we present only behavior state machines, which are widespread in practice and are also referred to as state machine diagrams or state charts.

In the same way as every other diagram, a state machine diagram only models the part of a system that is necessary or relevant for the respective purpose. For example, if you want to model only the states that a lecture hall can take, either for collecting requirements or for documentation purposes, a model as shown in Figure 5.1 can be sufficient. However, if you are already in a late phase of the development process, a representation that is close to code, as shown in Figure 5.2, is ben-

© Springer International Publishing Switzerland 2015
M. Seidl et al., *UML @ Classroom*, Undergraduate Topics
in Computer Science, DOI 10.1007/978-3-319-12742-2_5

eficial. This figure shows a class LectureHall with an attribute free that can take the values true and false. Calling the operation occupy sets free to false and the lecture hall object changes to the state free=false, which corresponds to the state occupied in Figure 5.1. The events in the state machine diagram are the equivalent of calling the respective operations of the class LectureHall.

Figure 5.2
State machine diagram, class diagram, and pseudocode of a lecture hall

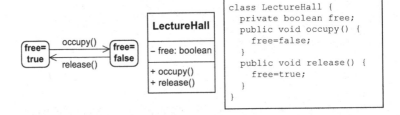

5.1 States and State Transitions

State

A state machine diagram is a graph with *states* as nodes and *state transitions* as edges. In the diagram, a state is shown as a rectangle with round corners and is labeled with the name of the state. When an object is in a specific state, all internal activities specified in this state can be executed by this object. If internal activities are specified for a state, it is divided into two compartments: the upper compartment of the rectangle contains the name of the state; the lower compartment includes *internal activities*, whereby an activity can consist of multiple actions. We will present the relationship between activities and actions in detail in Chapter 7, which looks at activity diagrams.

Internal activities

Within a state you can model three activities that are executed at a predefined moment. When an activity is specified after the keyword entry, this activity must then be executed when the object enters the state; conversely, the exit activity is executed when the object exits the state. An activity preceded by the keyword do is executed while the object remains in this state, that is, as long as this state is *active*. The respective activity is always specified with a prepended forward slash that clearly identifies it as an activity.

Figure 5.3 shows an extension of the example from Figure 5.1. As long as a lecture hall remains in the state free, that is, as long as the state free is active, the activity Display as available is executed and the lecture hall is displayed in the reservation system. If the lecture hall is occupied, it changes from the state free to the state occupied. At the moment the lecture hall enters this state, the activity Save user reservation is executed and the name of the person occupying the lecture hall is saved. While the lecture hall remains in the state occupied, the activity Display as occupied is executed. Once the lecture hall is no longer required, it is released and changes to the state free. When the lecture hall exits the state occupied, the activity Delete user reservation is executed.

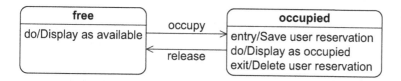

Figure 5.3
State machine diagram of a lecture hall with internal activities

The change from one state to another is referred to as a state transition or simply *transition*. A transition is represented with a directed edge, that is, an arrow. The arrowhead reflects the direction of the transition. The origin of the transition is referred to as the *source state* and the end of the transition is referred to as the *target state*. You can specify various properties for a transition:

Transition

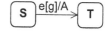

- The event (also called "trigger") that triggers the state transition
- The guard (also called "guard condition" or simply "condition") that enables the execution of the transition
- Activities (also called "effects") executed during the change to the target state

Synonyms:

- *Transition*
- *State transition*

Events are exogenous stimuli (that is, stimuli that come from outside the system/object) that can trigger a state transition. If the event specified for the transition occurs, the *guard* is checked. The guard is a boolean expression. At a specific point in time, it evaluates to either true or false. If the guard is true, all activities in the current state are terminated, any relevant exit activity is executed, and the transition takes place. During the state transition, any *activities* defined for that transition are executed. A transition—at least from a conceptual perspective—requires no time. Therefore, the system is always in a state and never in a transition. The activities specified for a transition must therefore also not require any significant time.

Event (Trigger)

Guard (Condition)

Activity (Effect)

If the guard evaluates to false, there is no state transition and the event is lost and not consumed. Even if the guard becomes true at a later point in time, the event must occur again for the transition to take place. If no guard is modeled at a transition, the default value [true] applies. If no event is specified at a transition, the transition is triggered when the entry activity and do activities of the current state are completed.

Completion event and
completion transition

Finishing these activities creates a *completion event* that triggers the transition. This type of transition is also referred to as a *completion transition*. If an event occurs for which no behavior is specified in the current state, the event is not consumed and is lost.

Guards are always set within square brackets to differentiate them from events and activities. Activities are always prepended with a forward slash (including activities in the states). Figure 5.4 illustrates the syntax of a transition specification.

Figure 5.4
Syntax of a transition
specification

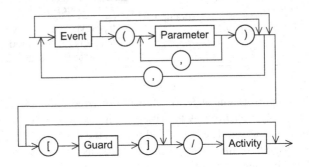

Internal transition ...

You can model *internal transitions* within states. These internal transitions handle the occurrence of events within a state. You use them to model the reaction to an event when the system does not exit the state that is currently active, meaning that entry and exit activities are not executed.

Figure 5.5 shows the two states that a student can take with reference to an exam, namely not registered and registered. As long as the student remains in the state not registered, every time a new exam date is published the student checks whether there is enough time to take the exam on this date—meaning that every time the event new date occurs the activity Check date is executed. If the event register occurs, provided the guard registration possible is true, the student switches to the state registered and the date of the exam is entered in the calendar. As long as the state registered is active, the student is studying. Any time the student encounters a problem, it is discussed with the student's colleagues. If the event withdraw occurs in the state registered, two different cases are possible. If the guard withdrawal possible is true, the activity Study for exam is interrupted and the student switches to the state not registered. When the student exits the state registered, the date is deleted from the calendar. However, if the guard withdrawal possible is false, the student remains in the state registered and must continue to study for the exam. (Believe it or not, in the home country of the authors it is possible to withdraw from an exam without consequences.)

... in contrast to
"external" transition

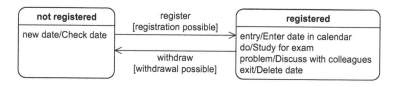

Figure 5.5
State machine diagram of
the registration status for
an exam

To further illustrate the concept of events, guards, and activities, Figure 5.6 shows abstract examples of transitions. The transition in Figure 5.6(a) has no event and no guard. Therefore the transition can take place as soon as A1 is completed. Figure 5.6(b) is similar to Figure 5.6(a) but activity A2 is executed during the transition. In Figure 5.6(c), the transition takes place as soon as event e1 occurs. If e1 occurs, the execution of the do activity A1 is immediately interrupted and the system switches to state S2. When the system exits state S1, the exit activity A2 is executed.

In Figure 5.6(d), guard g1 is checked as soon as e1 occurs. If the guard is true, A1 is terminated and there is a change of state to S2. If the guard is false, event e1 is lost and A1 is not interrupted. Figure 5.6(e) is similar to 5.6(d) but in 5.6(e), activity A2 is executed in addition during the transition.

Figure 5.6(f) shows an "unclean" use of a guard. The system stays in state S1 until A1 is completed. Guard g1 is not checked until this point and the transition takes place if g1 is true. If g1 is false, the system remains in state S1 and it will never be possible to exit S1 via this transition as the completion event of the do activity was lost when it was not consumed. This type of transition specification only makes sense if, for example, there is a further transition with a complementary guard, meaning that there is no dead end (not depicted here).

5.2 Types of States

In addition to the states discussed in Section 5.1, there are further types of state that enable you to model more complex content with state machine diagrams. There is a distinction between "real" states and *pseudostates*. Pseudostates are transient, which means that the system cannot remain in a pseudostate. They are not states in the actual sense but rather control structures that enable more complex states and state transitions. You cannot annotate activities to pseudostates. These pseudostates include the initial state, the decision node, the parallelization and synchronization nodes, the history state, the entry and exit points, and the terminate node. These are described in more detail below.

Pseudostates are transient

Figure 5.6
Examples of transitions

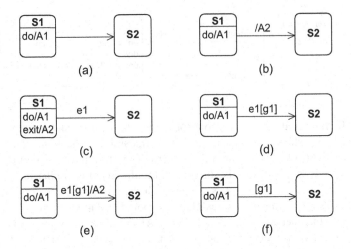

Initial state

The *initial state* is represented in the diagram as a small black circle and marks the "start" of a state machine diagram or a composite state (introduced in Section 5.5). The initial state has no incoming edges and usually one outgoing edge which leads to the first "real" state. If multiple outgoing edges are used, their guard conditions must be mutually exclusive and cover all possible cases to ensure that exactly one target state is reached. As soon as the system is in the initial state, it immediately—that is, without consuming any time—switches to the next state. Therefore, you cannot specify any events to the outgoing edge from the initial state. The only exception to this rule is the event that creates the modeled object itself—new() or create() for example. However, you can specify activities.

Decision node

The *decision node* is represented in the diagram with a diamond. You can use it to model alternative transitions. It has exactly one incoming edge and at least two outgoing edges. At the incoming edge, you model the event that triggers the transition; at the outgoing edges, you specify the guards for the alternative paths for the state transition. You can also specify activities at the incoming edge and all outgoing edges. If the event modeled at the incoming edge occurs, the system enters the transition. However, it pauses briefly at the decision node—but from a conceptual perspective without consuming any time—to evaluate the guards and thus select the outgoing edge to be used. To prevent the system getting "stuck" in the decision node, you must ensure that the guards cover all possible situations. Using [else] at one of the edges will allow you to do this. If the guards are not mutually exclusive, and if two or more edges are evaluated as true, one of these valid edges is selected nondeterministically. Figure 5.7(a) shows an example of the use of the decision node. If event e1 occurs, the transition takes place. Once the system has arrived at the decision node, the guards [b≤0] and [b>0] are evaluated and the system switches to state S2 or state S3. You can also model the same behavior without using a decision node, as shown in Figure 5.7(b). In contrast, Figure 5.7(c) and Figure 5.7(d) show different behavior. Figure 5.7(c) shows that if event e1 occurs, the transition starts and b is increased by the value 1. The guards are then evaluated. In Figure 5.7(d), b is only increased by the value 1 after the evaluation of the guards. Therefore, depending on the value of b, transitions to different states can occur in the two models. Figures 5.7(c) and 5.7(d) are therefore not semantically equivalent.

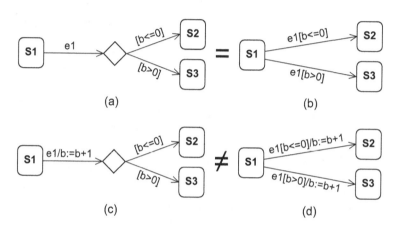

Figure 5.7
Modeling with and without decision nodes

Figure 5.8 shows the states that a student has when participating in a specific course. If the student is in the state not graded and the event grade occurs, depending on the grade the student receives, the student switches to the state positive or the state negative. The X in the model is called terminate node, which we will introduce later on in this chapter.

The *parallelization node* is represented with a black bar. It has exactly one incoming edge and at least two outgoing edges and is used to split the flow into multiple concurrent transitions. No events or guards may be specified at the outgoing edges of a parallelization node in a state machine diagram.

Parallelization node

The *synchronization node* is also represented with a black bar. It has at least two incoming edges and exactly one outgoing edge and is used to merge multiple concurrent flows. No events or guards may be specified at the incoming edges of a synchronization node. For more information on these two pseudostates and a description of the history state, see Section 5.5. Note that parallelization nodes must not be confused with decision nodes.

Synchronization node

Figure 5.8
States of a student's course
participation

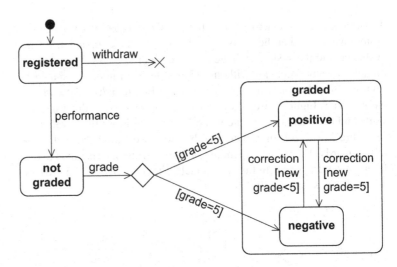

| Terminate node | The *terminate node* is represented in the diagram with a large X. |

Terminate node

The *terminate node* is represented in the diagram with a large X. If a terminate node is reached in a flow, the state machine terminates and the modeled object ceases to exist. In Figure 5.8, a specific course participation object for a certain student is deleted if it is in the state registered and the event withdraw occurs.

Final state ...

The only other "real" state—that is, a non-pseudostate—in addition to the states discussed in Section 5.1 is the *final state*. The final state has at least one incoming edge and no outgoing edges. In a diagram, it is represented by a small circle containing a solid circle. It marks the end of the sequence of states (see also Section 5.5). The object can remain in a final state permanently. Note that the final state must not be confused with the terminate node, where the modeled object is deleted! For a detailed explanation of entry and exit points, see Section 5.5.3.

... is a "real" state

5.3 Types of State Transitions

Internal transition

As already mentioned, there are two types of state transitions, namely internal transitions and external transitions. *Internal transitions* represent the reaction to an event that triggers an activity but not a state transition. As there is no change in state, no entry or exit activities are executed either. Entry and exit activities are modeled with the same notation as any other internal transition. However, they require the keywords entry and exit instead of the name of the triggering event in order to specify that the respective activity is executed when the system or object enters or exits the state. Internal transitions are modeled within states.

*Entry activity
and

exit activity*

When the system or object exits one state and enters another as a reaction to an event, the transition is called an *external transition*. First, the exit activities of the source state, then the activities of the transition, and finally the entry activities of the target state are executed as part of the state transition. A *self-transition* is a special type of external transition in which the source state and target state are identical.

External transition

Self-transition

Figure 5.9 shows examples of internal and external transitions.

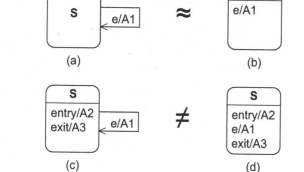

Figure 5.9
Examples of internal and external transitions

For example, Figure 5.9(b) shows an internal transition, Figure 5.9(e) an external transition, and Figure 5.9(a) a self-transition. The models in Figure 5.9(a) and Figure 5.9(b) show the same behavior: in both models, when event e occurs, activity A1 is executed; in both models, before event e occurs, the system was in state S just as it was after the processing of event e. Figures 5.9(c) and 5.9(d) are in no way equivalent, as in 5.9(c), whenever event e occurs, the system exits state S and thus exit activity A3 is executed, followed by A1, and finally, when the system again enters state S, entry activity A2 is executed. In contrast, in 5.9(d), event e does not trigger the exit and entry of state S, which is why no entry and exit activities are executed. If the same activity is modeled for all incoming transitions of a state, the execution of this activity can be modeled as an entry activity of the state instead. In the same way, activities for outgoing transitions can be modeled as an exit activity. Therefore, Figures 5.9(e) and 5.9(f) are semantically equivalent.

5.4 Types of Events

Signal event:
event name(arg1,arg2)

UML defines various types of events, with the most important being the signal event, call event, time event, change event, any receive event, and completion event. The *signal event* is used for asynchronous communication. In this case, a sender sends a signal to a receiver and does not wait for an answer. The receiver is the modeled object and the sender can be another object or the same object as the receiver. The receipt of the signal is processed as an event. The name of the event corresponds to that of the signal and arguments can be specified. For example, right-mouse-down or send sms(message) are signal events.

Call event:
opName(par1,par2)

Call events are operation calls. The name of the event corresponds to the name of an operation including parameters, for example, occupy(user,lectureHall) or register(exam).

Time event:
after(period)
when(time)

Time events enable time-based state transitions. The specified time can be relative—based on the time of the occurrence of the event in the state currently active—or absolute. Relative time events consist of the keyword after and a time span in parentheses, for example, after(5 seconds). Absolute time events are modeled with the keyword when and a time in parentheses, for example, expressions like when(time==16:00) or when(date==20150101) indicate absolute time events.

Change event:
when(boolExpr)

You can use a *change event* to permanently monitor whether a condition becomes true. A change event consists of a boolean expression in parentheses and the preceding keyword when. Examples of change events are when(registrations==number of seats) or when($x > y$). The event occurs as soon as the value of the logical expression changes from false to true. It is lost—just like every other event—if, for example, a guard prevents the event from being processed. However, it can only occur again when the value of the boolean expression changes from false to true again, meaning that the expression must have been false in the meantime. In Figure 5.10, the system is in the state course execution. As soon as semester end changes from false to true, the system checks whether grades are available. If this is the case, there is a state change to certificates issued. If no grades are available, the system remains in the state course execution and the change event is lost. Even if the guard [grades available] becomes true at a later point in time, there can be no transition. The system does not check the guard again until semester end has changed to false and then true again. This expresses that certificates can only be issued at the end of a semester, and then only if grades are available.

It is important to stress here that events of the type change event must not be confused with the guards for transitions. The system checks the boolean expression of a change event constantly and the event can trig-

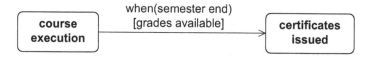

Figure 5.10
Example of a change event

ger a state transition in the instant it becomes true. In contrast, a guard is only evaluated when the related event occurs. Therefore, a guard can never trigger an event itself. In Figure 5.11 a small example illustrates this difference. A student can be in one of two states, namely attending lecture or leisure time. In (a), the student listens to the lecture for 90 minutes. After 90 minutes, there is a state transition to the state leisure time. In contrast, in (b), the student listens until the end of the lecture, as it is only when the event lecture ended occurs that the system checks whether the lecture has already lasted for 90 minutes. If we model the content as shown in (a), this means that leisure time begins for the student after exactly 90 minutes. According to model (b), leisure time begins whenever the lecturer finishes the lecture—but at the earliest after 90 minutes, as the guard is only true then. Note that this model assumes that the lecture is never shorter than 90 minutes.

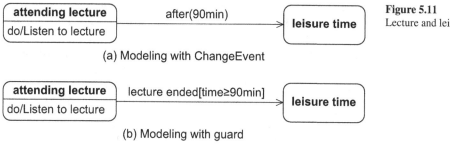

Figure 5.11
Lecture and leisure time

You can use an *any receive event* to specify a type of "else" transition. For this type of event, the keyword all is attached to a transition as an event which occurs when any event occurs that does not trigger another transition for the active state. In Figure 5.12, the system changes from state S1 to state S2 if event e1 occurs. If e2 occurs, there is a transition to state S3. If any other event occurs, the system changes to S4.

*Any receive event:
all*

A *completion event* takes place when everything to be done in the current state is completed. This includes entry and do activities as well as the completion of nested states, if there are any (see next Section). If a state has an outgoing transition without any event specified, the completion event triggers this transition.

Completion event

Figure 5.12
Transition with any receive
event

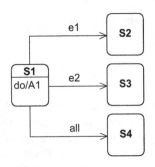

5.5 Composite States

Composite state ...

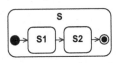

... consists of substates

*Arbitrary nesting depth
of substates*

Synonyms:

- *Composite state*
- *Complex state*
- *Nested state*

A simple state consists only of internal and external transitions and entry, do and exit activities, if there are any. It has no further substructure.
A *composite state*, also referred to as a *complex state* or a *nested state*,
is a state that contains multiple other states as well as pseudostates. The
states contained within a composite state are referred to as its *substates*.
A composite state can have an initial state. A transition to the boundary of this composite state can be understood as an implicit transition
to the initial state of the composite state. If multiple states are nested
within one another, that is, if a composite state contains further composite states, which in turn also contain further composite states, and so
on, the life cycle of a new object always begins at the outermost initial
state. The same applies for the final state. If a composite state has a final
state, a transition that leads to this final state creates a completion event
of the composite state in which the final state is located. Alternatively,
transitions can lead to or away from a substate of a composite state.

Figure 5.13 shows examples of how a composite state can be entered
or exited. If an object is in state S3 and event e2 occurs, composite state
S1 becomes active and the initial state of S1 is entered. This triggers
the immediate transition to state S1.1. However, if e1 occurs while the
object is in S3, state S1.2 becomes active. If the object is in state S1.2
and e4 occurs, the object exits the higher level state S1, the assigned
completion transition is executed, and the corresponding target state S2
is activated. However, if e3 occurs while the object is in state S1.1, the
object immediately changes to state S2 and does not reach S1.2.

If e3 occurs while the object is in state S1.2, the system remains in
S1.2 and the event is lost because it is neither consumed within S1.2,
nor is the event specified on a transition originating from S1.2 or the
states it is contained in.

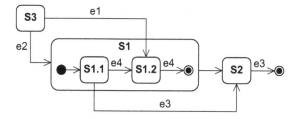

Figure 5.13
Example of the entry into
and exit from a composite
state

5.5.1 The Orthogonal State

If a composite state is active, only one of its substates is active at any
point in time. If you want to achieve concurrent states, a composite state
can be divided into two or more regions, whereby one state of each region is always active at any point in time. This type of composite state
is called an *orthogonal state*. Each region of an orthogonal state can
have an initial state. A transition to the boundary of the orthogonal state
then activates the initial states of all regions. Each region can also have
a final state. In this case, the completion event of the higher level state
is not created until the final state is reached in all regions. If an orthogonal state is not to be entered or exited via its initial states and final
states, the parallelization and synchronization nodes presented briefly
in Section 5.2 are required. The incoming edge of the parallelization
node may show events, guards, and activities, but at the outgoing edges,
only activities are permitted. Every outgoing edge must target a substate of a different region of the same orthogonal state. Conversely, all
edges that end in a synchronization node must originate from substates
of different regions of the same orthogonal state. The outgoing edge of
a synchronization node may show events, guards, and activities, but at
the incoming edges, only activities are permitted.

Orthogonal state

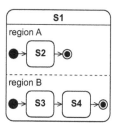

Figure 5.14 shows an example of how an orthogonal state can be
entered or exited. If S1 is entered via state S2, the initial states of the
two orthogonal regions region A and region B are activated. However, if
S1 is entered via the transition that proceeds from S3, SA2 and SB2 are
activated. There are four different ways of exiting state S1. If the final
state has been reached in both regions, a completion event is created
and there is a completion transition to S4 via the "bare" edge. If event
e3 occurs while the object is in any substate of S1, any ongoing activities in S1 are terminated, the object exits all substates of S1, and there
is an immediate transition to S5. If all activities in SA3 and SB3 were
completed before events e1 and e2 occurred, there is a transition to S5.
Event e4 offers the final opportunity to exit S1. If the system is in state
SA2 and event e4 occurs, any ongoing activities in S1 are terminated,

the object exits all substates of S1, and there is a transition to state S4. This takes place regardless of which state of region B the object was in at the time the event e4 occurred.

Figure 5.14
Example of the entry into and exit from an orthogonal state

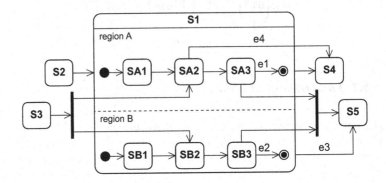

5.5.2 Submachines

If multiple state machine diagrams share parts with the same behavior, it is not practical to model the same behavior multiple times, because this would make the models difficult to maintain and reuse. In this situation, the recommendation is to reuse parts of state machine diagrams in other

Submachine   state machine diagrams. To do this, you model the behavior that is to be reused in a *submachine* accessed from another state machine diagram by

Submachine state   a *submachine state*. A submachine is a special type of composite state. The name of the submachine state takes the form state:submachine state.

S:SMS ○–○   In addition, you can optionally annotate the submachine state with a

Refinement symbol refinement symbol. If a submachine state is modeled in a state machine

○–○   diagram, as soon as the submachine state is activated, the behavior of the submachine is executed. This is equivalent to calling a subroutine

Submachine ≅   in programming languages. If there is a transition to the boundary of

subroutine   the submachine state, the initial state of the referenced submachine is activated. If a final state is reached in the submachine, the state of the calling state machine diagram that the transition from the submachine state leads to is activated. Figure 5.15 shows the states that a student can take when participating in a specific course, whereby the modeling of the states positive and negative has been transferred to the submachine grade, which is referenced in the state graded.

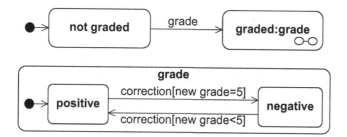

Figure 5.15
The states of a student in a
course

5.5.3 Entry and Exit Points

If a composite state shall be entered or exited via a state other than the
initial and final states, you can model this using *entry* and *exit points*. An
entry point is modeled by a small circle at the boundary of the composite state and has a name that describes the entry point. The entry point
has a transition to the state where the execution should begin. If an external transition leads to this entry point, the execution can be started
with the desired state without the external transition having to know the
structure of the composite state. If the composite state is not to be ended
as usual when the final state is reached but instead through the ending of
another state, you can model exit points in the same way. An exit point
is denoted at the boundary of the composite state by a small circle containing an X and has a name that describes the exit point. If an external
transition has the exit point as source state, this relates to the alternatively determined final state but without the external transition having
to know the structure of the composite state. Entry and exit points are
therefore a type of encapsulation mechanism. In practice, they are used
in particular when modeling and using submachines.

    Figure 5.16(a) shows a modification of the example from Figure 5.13.
Instead of the transition leading directly to S1.2, an entry point is used.
In the same way, S1.1 is exited via an exit point. Figure 5.16(b) shows
the external view of S1. The entry and exit points are visible as interfaces to S1 but the detailed structure of S1 remains invisible for external
transitions.

Entry point

Exit point

*Composite state with
entry and exit point*

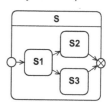

Figure 5.16
Example of entering and
exiting a composite state
with entry and exit points
(see Fig. 5.13)

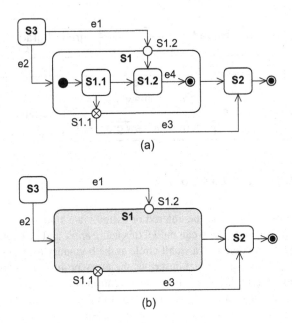

(a)

(b)

Figure 5.17 shows a modification of the example from Figure 5.8, in
which the substates of the state graded are entered via entry points. Thus
outside the state graded, no internal details of graded have to be known.

Figure 5.17
Modeling of the example
from Figure 5.8 with entry
points

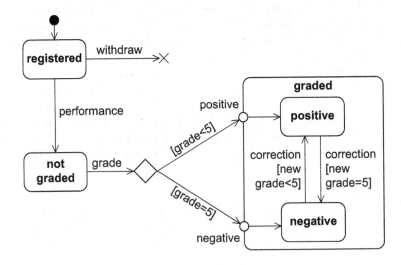

5.5.4 The History State

History states are used when, after an external transition that leads away from a composite state, the system is to return to the same substate that was active before the transition occurred. The history state remembers which substate of a composite state was last active. If a transition from outside leads to the history state, the history state activates the "old" substate and all entry activities are conducted sequentially from the outside to the inside of the complex state. A history state can have any number of incoming edges but only one outgoing edge. The outgoing edge must not have any events or guards. Its target is the substate that is to be active if the composite state was never active before and there is therefore no "last active substate", or if the composite state was recently exited in the "standard way" via the final state being reached.

History state

There are two types of history states: the *shallow history state* and the *deep history state*. Every composite state may have a maximum of one shallow history state and one deep history state. The shallow history state restores the state that is on the same level of the composite state as the shallow history state itself. In contrast, the deep history state notes the last active substate over the entire nesting depth.

Shallow history state

Figure 5.18 illustrates the difference between the shallow and the deep history states with an example.

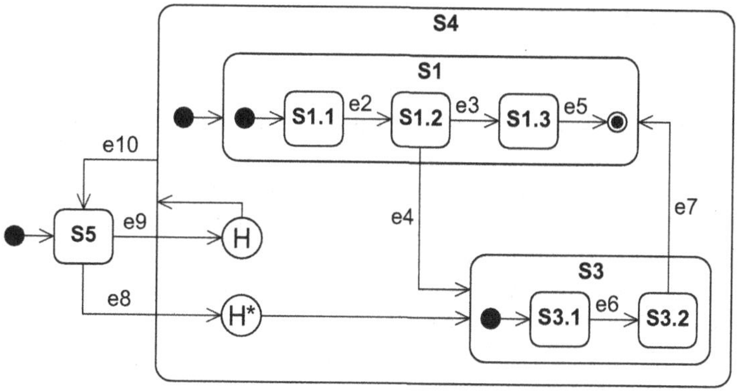

Deep history state

Figure 5.18
Shallow history state and
deep history state

Let us assume that the object is in state S1 and there in substate S1.2 when e10 occurs and forces a transition to S5. The shallow history state remembers that the object was previously in state S1 because S1 is on the same level as the shallow history state itself. In contrast, the deep history state remembers that the last active state was actually S1.2, as it knows the position over the entire nesting depth. If event e8 occurs, the deep history state activates state S1.2. However, if e9 occurs instead, the shallow history state activates state S1 and, therefore, the initial state of S1 is active, which immediately activates the first real state, S1.1. Let us now assume that state S4 in the life cycle of our object has never been active and the object is currently in state S5. If e8 now occurs, the deep history state activates state S3 and thus implicitly S3.1, as the outgoing edge of the deep history state points to S3. If e9 occurs instead, the edge of the shallow history state points to the boundary of S4 and therefore the initial state of S4 is activated. In turn, this activates S1, which, via its initial state, activates the first real state, S1.1.

Figure 5.19 shows the states that a student takes during a study program. Initially, a study program is inactive. If the tuition fees have been paid (and thus the student has registered for the study program), the study program becomes active. Tuition fees must be paid at the beginning of every semester. If this does not happen, the study program becomes inactive again. During the course of an active study program, the student progresses through the levels bachelor, master, and doctorate. If the student does not pay the tuition fees for a particular semester—for example, because the student wants to take a break for one semester—after this semester, it should be possible for the student to return to the stage of the study program that was reached before the break. The deep history state ensures that this is possible.

5.6 Sequence of Events

In a final example, we will illustrate the relation of events, guards, and activities in states and in state transitions. Special attention is given to the order in which activities are executed.

Figure 5.20 shows an abstract example of a state machine diagram. Depending on which events occur, there are different state transitions. The variables x, y, and z are set to different values during the execution of certain activities. We will use the example to solve the following question: What state is the state machine in after the occurrences of the events e2, e1, e3, e4, e1, and e5 (in that given order) and what values are the variables x, y, and z set to?

At the beginning, the state machine is in state A, whereby before the entry into state A, the variable x was assigned the value 2. When the state machine enters state A, variable z is set to the value 0. The system now remains in state A until event e2—the first event in this specific example—occurs. As soon as e2 occurs, the state machine exits state A. When the state machine exits A, the value of z is increased by the value 1; z is therefore 1. There is a transition to state C. As part of this transition, the value of z is multiplied by 2; z is therefore 2. When

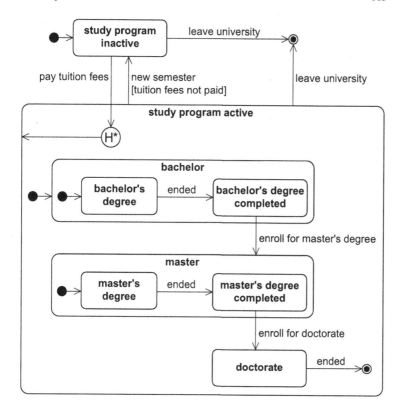

Figure 5.19
States of an academic
education

the state machine enters composite state C, z is increased by 1 again and now has the value 3. Furthermore, y is set to the value 2. The initial state of composite state C leads directly to state C1; when the state machine enters C1, z is again multiplied by 2 and now has the value 6.

If e1 now occurs, the state machine remains in state C1, as this event occurrence "only" triggers an internal transition and is processed within C1. The variable x is set to the value 4. Then e3 occurs, and the system checks which value z has at this point in time. As z currently has the value 6, the guard [z==6] is true. When the state machine exits C1, z is set to the value 3 and there is a state transition to state C2. When the state machine enters C2, y is set to 0. The next event in the sequence is e4, and therefore the state machine exits C2 and the exit activity of C2 is executed; x therefore becomes -1. The state machine then exits composite state C and this state's exit activity is executed. The variable y is set to the value 1. When the state machine then enters E, y is increased by the value 1. The variable y therefore becomes 2. The occurrence of event e1 makes the state machine exit state E. The history state returns to the last active substate of C, that is, to C2. As a result of the execution

Figure 5.20
State machine diagram to
demonstrate a sequence of
events

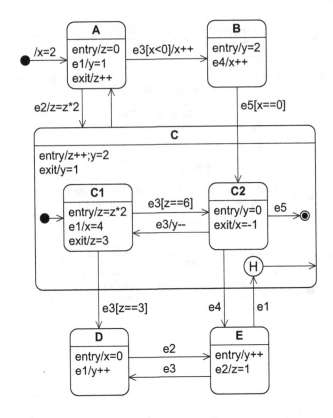

of the entry activities of C, the value of z increases from 3 to 4 and y is
set to the value 2. The execution of the entry activity of C2 means that
y is overwritten with the value 0. The last event in this example is e5.
This event leads the state machine to the final state of composite state
C. When the state machine exits C2, x is set to the value -1, which is
irrelevant as x already has this value. There is an edge that leads away
from state C where no event is specified at this edge. The completion
event created by the ending of C thus leads to a completion transition
to state A via this "empty" edge. When the state machine exits C, y is
set to the value 1. When the state machine then enters A, z is set to 0.
Therefore, after the events e2, e1, e3, e4, e1, and e5, our state machine
is in state A, x has the value −1, y is 1, and z has the value 0. Table 5.1
summarizes the individual steps.

Event	State entered	x	y	z
Start	A	2		0
e2	C1		2	6
e1	C1	4		
e3	C2		0	3
e4	E	-1	2	
e1	C2		0	4
e5	A	-1	1	0

Table 5.1
State changes and variable assignments for x, y, and z after the occurrence of the individual events

5.7 Summary

A state machine diagram can be used to show the states in which a system or an object can find itself during its "life cycle", that is, from its creation to its destruction. The diagram also shows the conditions under which the transitions between these states occur. Events and activities triggered by these events can be modeled in the diagram. You can also specify guards that must apply for an event to trigger related activities or a state transition. Additional concepts allow you to model more complex state machine diagrams. Parallelization and synchronization nodes, as well as orthogonal states, enable you to model simultaneously active states and chains of states. The shallow and deep history states, as well as entry and exit points, allow a defined entry into transitive nested substates of composite states. The most important elements of the state machine diagram are summarized in Table 5.2.

Table 5.2
Notation elements for the
state machine diagram

Name	Notation	Description
State	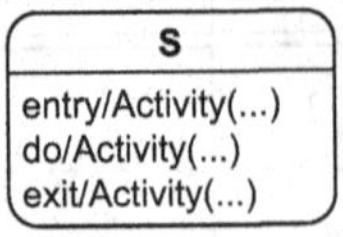 S entry/Activity(...) do/Activity(...) exit/Activity(...)	Description of a specific "time span" in which an object finds itself during its "life cycle". Within a state, activities can be executed on the object.
Transition	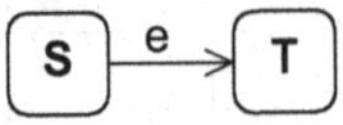 S e T	State transition e from a source state S to a target state T
Initial state	●	Start of a state machine diagram
Final state	◉	End of a state machine diagram
Terminate node	✕	Termination of an object's state machine diagram
Decision node	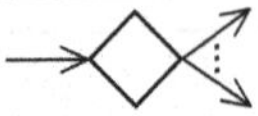 ◇	Node from which multiple alternative transitions can proceed
Parallelization node	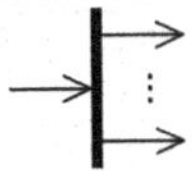	Splitting of a transition into multiple parallel transitions
Synchronization node	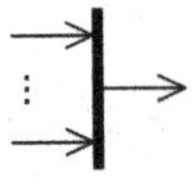	Merging of multiple parallel transitions into one transition
Shallow and deep history state	 (H) / (H*)	"Return address" to a substate or a nested substate of a composite state

Chapter 6
The Sequence Diagram

While the purpose of the state machine diagram presented in the last chapter is to model the *intra*-object behavior—that is, the life cycle of an object—in this chapter we look at the modeling of the *inter*-object behavior—that is, the interactions between the objects in a system.

Intra-object behavior versus inter-object behavior

An *interaction* specifies how messages and data are exchanged between interaction partners. The *interaction partners* are either human, such as lecturers or students, or non-human, such as a server, a printer, or executable software. An interaction can be a conversation between multiple persons—for example, an oral exam. Alternatively, an interaction can model communication protocols such as HTTP or represent the message exchange between humans and a software system—for example, between a lecturer and the student administration system when the lecturer publishes exam results. An interaction can also be a sequence of method calls in a program or signals such as a fire alarm and the resulting communication processes.

Interaction
Interaction partner

An interaction describes the interplay between multiple interaction partners and comprises a sequence of *messages*. The sending or receipt of a message can be triggered by the occurrence of certain events, for example, the receipt of another message, and can take place at specified times, for example, at 05:00. Predefined constraints specify any necessary preconditions that must be met for successful interactions. For example, continuing the communication process outlined above, the lecturer must be logged into the system before entering the students' grades.

Message

In UML, you use *interaction diagrams* to specify interactions. In an interaction diagram, you always model a concrete scenario, meaning that the message exchange takes place within a specific context to fulfill a specific task. Interactions usually only describe a specific part of a situation. There are often other valid execution paths that the interaction

Interaction diagram

© Springer International Publishing Switzerland 2015
M. Seidl et al., *UML @ Classroom*, Undergraduate Topics
in Computer Science, DOI 10.1007/978-3-319-12742-2_6

diagram does not cover. Although data exchanged through the messages and processed or stored by the interaction partners can be represented in interaction diagrams, the purpose of modeling interactions is not to specify exactly how this data is to be manipulated. If required, you can add this type of information to interaction diagrams, but other diagrams such as the activity diagram (see Chapter 7) would take preference to model this information.

Interactions offer a mechanism for describing communication sequences at different levels of detail, both for computer experts as well as for end users and decision-makers. Interaction diagrams are therefore

Use of interaction diagrams   used in various situations. For example, they are used to represent the interaction of a complete system with its environment. In this case, the system can be interpreted as a black box of which only the interfaces visible to the outside are known. You can also use interaction diagrams to model the interaction between system parts in order to show how a specific use case (see Chapter 3) can be implemented. In late design phases, you can use interaction diagrams to precisely model interprocess communication in which the partners involved must observe certain protocols. Interaction diagrams can also zoom in much further into the system to be realized and can model communication at class level, meaning that you can use them to model operation calls and inter-object behavior.

Of the four interaction diagrams offered by UML, the sequence diagram is the one most frequently used—often in an informal way to quickly present interaction sequences. However, in this chapter, we describe the elements of the sequence diagram in detail and examine how to apply them according to the UML standard. In Section 6.7 we briefly introduce the other three interaction diagrams and compare them to the sequence diagram.

6.1 Interaction Partners

Lifeline   In a sequence diagram, the interaction partners are depicted as *lifelines*.

A lifeline is shown as a vertical, usually dashed line that represents the lifetime of the object associated with it (see Fig. 6.1). At the top end of the line is the head of the lifeline, a rectangle which contains an expression in the form roleName:Class (Fig. 6.1(c)). This expression indicates the name of the role and the class of the object associated with the lifeline. In the same way as for the object diagram (see Chapter 4.1 on page 50), one of the two names may be omitted. If you omit the class, you can omit the colon (Fig. 6.1(a)); however, if you specify only the class, the colon must precede the class name (Fig. 6.1(b)). Thus you can define a sequence diagram at both instance level and class level.

You can also use other symbols for interaction partners instead of the rectangle, for example the stick figure that we saw in the use case diagram for actors (see Chapter 3).

In a sequence diagram, the use of the role concept allows more modeling flexibility than simple instances or classes. An object—that is, an instance of a class—can take on different *roles* over its lifetime. In our university system, it is quite conceivable that the person helenLewis is initially only a student, who then becomes a tutor, and finally a professor. With each new role, there are certain activities that Helen Lewis is no longer permitted to perform or no longer has to perform. However, there are other activities that she is now allowed to perform instead. If we considered only the class of the object helenLewis to reflect the different roles that the object can take, every time the role of the object changed we would have to delete the object and create a new one. Alternatively, the class would have to be changed dynamically.

Role

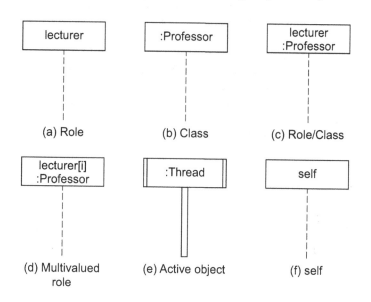

(a) Role   (b) Class   (c) Role/Class

(d) Multivalued role   (e) Active object   (f) self

Figure 6.1
Types of lifelines

Roles can also be connected to more than one object. This type of role is referred to as a *multivalued role*. However, a lifeline may only represent one specific object. This object is selected by a *selector*. The selector is specified in square brackets between the role name and the colon. It can be formulated in any language, for example in natural language, pseudocode, or Java. In the example in Figure 6.1(d), the selector is simply a variable that acts as an index. To specify multiple objects of

Multivalued role

Selector

a role as independent interaction partners simultaneously, you must assign each object to a separate lifeline.

Active object

A lifeline can represent an *active object*. Active objects are used to model processes and threads. An active object has its own control flow, meaning that it can operate independently of other objects. The head of a lifeline that represents an active object has a double boundary on the left and right. A continuous bar is often used instead of the dashed line (see Fig. 6.1(e)).

In Figure 6.1(f), the head of the lifeline contains the name self. This is needed when a class spans a certain interaction context and is itself involved in the interaction.

6.2 Exchanging Messages

The sequence diagram is a two-dimensional diagram (see Fig. 6.2). The interaction partners involved in the interaction are presented on the horizontal axis and should be arranged in a clear order. The vertical axis models the chronological order of the interaction. If the chronological order has not been explicitly set aside, an event further up on the vertical axis takes place before an event that is lower down on the vertical axis—provided both events refer to the same lifeline.

Event specification

In a sequence diagram, interactions are considered as a sequence of *event specifications*. Event specifications cover the sending and receipt of messages or the occurrence of time-based events such as a point in

Figure 6.2
Structure of a sequence
diagram

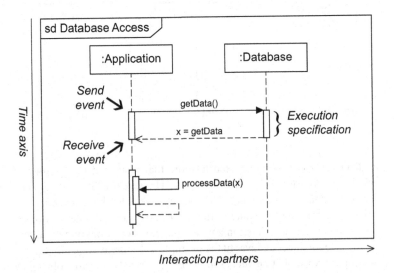

time, for example. The vertical time axis determines the sequence of event occurrences on a lifeline, although this does not define the order of event occurrences on different lifelines. An order across multiple lifelines is only forced if messages are exchanged between the different lifelines. Unless specified otherwise, below we assume that the message transmission does not require any time, meaning that the send event at the sender and the receive event at the receiver take place at the same time. This allows us to present the traces more compactly because we do not have to consider sequences of send and receive events and can concentrate on sequences of messages. The chronological connection between a message a and a message b is expressed by the symbol →. For example, a → b means that message a is sent before message b. Figure 6.3 summarizes possible message sequences. If the send and receive events of two messages take place along the same lifeline, the chronological order of these events determines the order of the messages. In Figure 6.3(a), message a must always take place before message c, as the send event of a takes place before the send event of c. If two messages do not have any common interaction partners, the order of these messages is not specified. In Figure 6.3(b), this is the case for messages a and c. There are therefore two possible traces: a → c and c → a. If a message b is inserted between a and c and this message forces a and c into a chronological order, the only possible trace is a → b → c (see Fig. 6.3(c)).

Send event and receive event

Trace

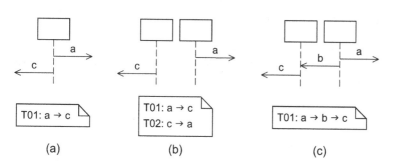

Figure 6.3
Sequences of messages and possible traces

(a) (b) (c)

The execution of behavior is indicated by two events that start and finish this execution on the same lifeline (see Fig. 6.2). This behavior is visualized with a bar and is referred to as an *execution specification*. The authors of the book UML@Work [23] differentiate between *direct* and *indirect* execution behavior. In the case of direct execution, the interaction partner affected executes the specified behavior itself; with indirect execution, the interaction partner delegates the execution to other interaction partners. Overlapping execution specifications are shown with overlapping bars. If an interaction partner sends a message to itself and

Execution specification

Direct versus indirect execution

Message to self

the associated execution specification is to be modeled explicitly, two
bars of execution specifications are shown overlapping, whereby the
message arrow points to the second bar, and in the case of a synchronous
message, a dashed response arrow at the end of the execution leads back
to the original bar (see processData(x) in Fig. 6.2).

You do not have to model execution specifications—they are optional
and are mainly used to visualize when an interaction partner executes
some behavior. Many UML tools draw the corresponding bars automatically as continuous bars from the first to the last message that affects
an interaction partner. For reasons of clarity, in this book we generally
do not show execution specifications in our sequence diagrams.

6.3 Messages

Message

Synchronous message

Asynchronous message

Response message

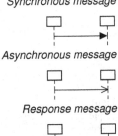

In a sequence diagram, a *message* is depicted as an arrow from the
sender to the receiver. The type of the arrow expresses the type of communication involved. A *synchronous message* is represented by an arrow with a continuous line and a filled triangular arrowhead. An *asynchronous message* is depicted by an arrow with a continuous line and an
open arrowhead. In the case of synchronous messages, the sender waits
until it has received a *response message* before continuing. The response
message is represented by a dashed line with an open arrowhead. If the
content of the response message and the point at which the response
message is sent and received are clear from the context, then the response message may be omitted in the diagram. In asynchronous communication, the sender continues after having sent the message. Two
examples are shown in Figure 6.4.

Figure 6.4
Examples of (a) asyn-
chronous and (b) syn-
chronous communication

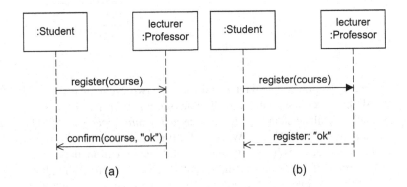

In both cases, a student is communicating with a professor in order to register for a course. In case (a), the registration is via e-mail, that is, asynchronous. The student does not explicitly wait for the receipt of the confirmation message. In case (b), the student registers with the professor personally and the communication is therefore synchronous. The student waits until receiving a response message.

Messages are identified by a name, with the optional specification of parameters and a return value (see Fig. 6.5). The parameters are separated by commas and are enclosed within parentheses. The return value can optionally be assigned to a variable as well. Thus, a message can be labeled with var=m1:value, whereby var is the variable to which the return value is to be assigned, m1 specifies the name of the message, and value represents the actual return value.

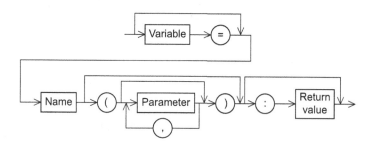

Figure 6.5
Syntax of the message specification

The receipt of a message by an object generally calls the corresponding operation specified in the class diagram (see Chapter 4). In principle, the passed arguments should be compatible with the parameters of the operation specification in the class diagram (see Fig. 4.8 on page 57). However, if you use parameter names to assign the values to the corresponding parameters, neither the number nor the order of the arguments has to match the parameters in the operation specification.

A *message for creating objects* is a special type of message. It is depicted by a dashed arrow with an open arrowhead that ends at the head of the lifeline associated with the object to be created. The arrow is labeled with the keyword new and corresponds to calling a constructor in an object-oriented programming language. For example, in Figure 6.6, a Professor creates a new ExamDate.

Create message

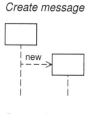

If an object is deleted during the course of an interaction, that is, a *destruction event* occurs, the end of the lifeline is marked with a large X (see Fig. 6.6). Otherwise a lifeline stretches to the lower end of the sequence diagram.

Destruction event

Figure 6.6
Creation of an object

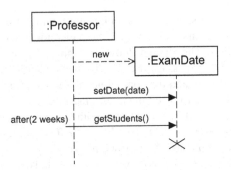

Found message

If the sender of a message is unknown or not relevant, you can express this with *found messages*. In this case, you use a black circle as source instead of specifying an interaction partner that sends the message. In Figure 6.7, the sender of the message spamEmail is unknown.

Figure 6.7
Example of lost and found
messages

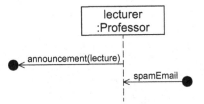

Lost message

The counterpart to the found message is the *lost message*. With this type of message, it is the receiver that is unknown or not relevant. The receiver is also noted as a black circle. The lecture announcement in Figure 6.7 is sent to an arbitrary (and therefore unknown or irrelevant) receiver.

Time-consuming
message

Synonyms:

- *Time-consuming*
  message
- *Message with*
  duration

Up to this point, we have implicitly assumed that the messages are transmitted without any loss of time. Of course, this is not always the case. If you want to express that time elapses between the sending and the receipt of a message, you model the message as a diagonal line in the sequence diagram rather than a horizontal line. As the time dimension is represented vertically, this visualizes the duration required for the transmission of a message. This type of message is referred to as a *time-consuming message* or *message with duration*.

Figure 6.8 shows an example scenario. A student enrolls for a study program in the student administration system. Within the next two to three days, the student receives a confirmation message affirming that the enrollment was successful. This confirmation is sent as a traditional letter and is therefore in transit for a few days before the student receives it.

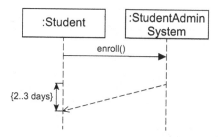

Figure 6.8
Example of a time-
consuming message

6.4 Combined Fragments

In a sequence diagram, you can use *combined fragments* (operators) to
model various control structures explicitly. This enables you to describe
a number of possible execution paths compactly and precisely. Within
a diagram, a combined fragment is represented by a rectangle, with the
operator type specified by the respective keyword in a small pentagon
in the upper left corner of this rectangle. UML offers 12 different types
of operators. Depending on the type of the operator, it contains one
or multiple operands which can in turn contain interactions, combined
fragments, or references to other sequence diagrams. Different operands
of an operator are separated from one another by horizontal, dashed
lines. Gates describe the interfaces between a combined fragment and
its environment (see Section 6.5.2).

In [23], the 12 different types of operators are split into three groups:

- Branches and loops
- Concurrency and order
- Filters and assertions

Table 6.1 provides an overview of the available operators with the
corresponding keywords and their semantics. In the following, we refer
to the different fragments according to their operator—for example, a
combined fragment with an alt operator is referred to simply as an alt
fragment.

Combined fragment

Operator

Operands

Combined fragments can be nested arbitrarily, whereby a frame is
specified for each fragment. Alternatively, nested fragments may share
a frame. If this is the case, in the pentagon in the upper left corner of the
frame, the corresponding keywords are specified separated by a space.
The operator to the furthest left is assigned to the outermost fragment,
and the operator to the furthest right is assigned to the innermost fragment (see Fig. 6.9).

Table 6.1
Operators for combined
fragments

	Operator	Purpose
Branches and loops	alt	Alternative interaction
	opt	Optional interaction
	loop	Iterative interaction
	break	Exception interaction
Concurrency and order	seq	Weak order
	strict	Strict order
	par	Concurrent interaction
	critical	Atomic interaction
Filters and assertions	ignore	Irrelevant interaction parts
	consider	Relevant interaction parts
	assert	Asserted interaction
	neg	Invalid interaction

6.4.1 Branches and Loops

alt fragment

Alternative interaction

Guard

Predefined guard else

You can use an alt fragment to represent alternative sequences. An alt operator has at least two operands. Each operand represents an alternative path in the execution, which corresponds approximately to multiple cases in programming languages, for example, the `switch` statement in Java. Guards are used to select the path to be executed.

Each operand has a *guard*. A guard is a boolean expression enclosed within square brackets. If there is no guard, then [true] is assumed as the default value. If multiple guards are true simultaneously, this results in an indeterminism. In this case, there is no prediction regarding which operand is selected. This contrasts with the semantics of switch statements in common programming languages, in which the alternatives are usually processed from top to bottom. A special guard is [else], which is evaluated as true if no other condition is fulfilled. If none of the guards evaluates to true, no operand is executed and the execution of the surrounding fragment continues. Figure 6.10 shows an example of the alt

Figure 6.9
Notation alternatives for
nested combined fragments

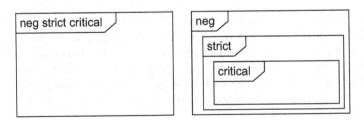

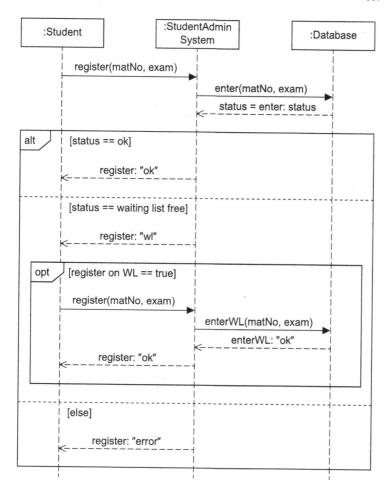

Figure 6.10
Example of an alt and an
opt fragment

fragment. When a student wants to register for an exam, the following cases can occur: (1) There are still places available and the student can register. (2) There is a place available on the waiting list. Then the student has to decide whether to go on the waiting list. (3) If there is no place available for the exam or on the waiting list for the exam, the student receives an error message and is not registered for the course.

The opt fragment corresponds to an alt fragment with two operands, one of which is empty. The opt operator thus represents an interaction sequence whose actual execution at runtime is dependent on the guard. In a programming language, this operator would be specified as an `if` statement without an `else` branch. Figure 6.10 illustrates the use of the opt fragment. If there is a place available on the waiting list, when registering for an assignment the student can decide whether to take the

opt fragment

Optional interaction

place on the waiting list. If the student wants to be on the waiting list, the student has to register for it.

loop fragment
Repeated interaction

You can use the loop fragment to express that a sequence is to be executed repeatedly. This combined fragment has exactly one operand. The keyword loop is followed by an optional specification of the number of iterations of the loop. This specification takes the form (min..max) or (min,max), where min specifies the minimum number of iterations that the loop must go through and max denotes the maximum number of iterations. If min and max are identical, you can omit one of the two numbers and the dots. If there is no upper limit to the number of loop iterations, you only need to specify an asterisk ∗. In this case, the minimum number of iterations is assumed to be zero. If the keyword loop is not followed by any further specification of the number of iterations, ∗ is assumed as the default value. If required, you can specify a guard, which is then checked for each iteration within the (min,max) limits. This means that the guard is evaluated as soon as the minimum number of iterations has taken place. If the underlying condition is not fulfilled, the execution of the loop is terminated even if the maximum number of executions has not yet been reached. Figure 6.11 expands the example from Figure 6.10 to include the system login that is necessary before a student can register for an assignment. The password must be entered at least once and at most three times, as reflected by the arguments of loop. After the first attempt, the system checks whether the password can be validated. If it can, that is, the condition Password incorrect is no longer true, execution of the interactions within the loop ceases. The system also exits the loop if the student enters the password incorrectly three times. This case is then handled further in the subsequent break fragment.

break fragment
Exception handling

The break fragment has the same structure as an opt operator, that is, it consists of a single operand plus a guard. If the guard is true, the interactions within this operand are executed, the remaining operations of the surrounding fragment are omitted, and the interaction continues in the next higher level fragment. The break operator thus offers a simple form of exception handling. For our example in Figure 6.11, this means that if the password is entered incorrectly three times, the condition incorrect password is true. Thus the content of the break fragment is executed, meaning that an error message is sent to the student and the student is not allowed to register for the assignment. The remainder of the interaction after the end of the break fragment is skipped. After exiting the break operator, we are in the outermost fragment of the sequence diagram and therefore the execution of this sequence diagram is ended. If we were not in the outermost fragment, the sequence diagram would continue in the fragment at the next higher level.

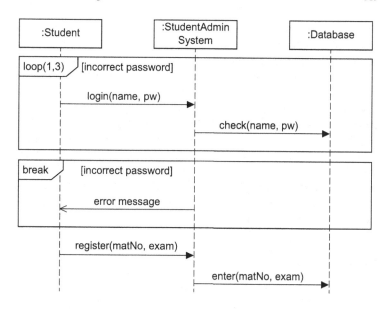

Figure 6.11
Example of a **break** and
loop fragment

6.4.2 Concurrency and Order

As already discussed, the arrangement of events on the vertical axis represents the chronological order of these events, provided there is a message exchange between the interaction partners involved. The combined fragments described below allow you to explicitly control the order of event occurrences.

The **seq** fragment represents the default order. It has at least one operand and expresses weak sequencing which is specified by the UML standard [35] as follows:

seq fragment

Sequential interaction with weak order

1. The ordering of events within each of the operands is maintained in the result.
2. Events on different lifelines from different operands may come in any order.
3. Events on the same lifeline from different operands are ordered such that an event of the first operand comes before that of the second operand.

We can use the seq fragment to group messages together with a break fragment. If the condition of the break fragment becomes true, the messages from the seq fragment that have not yet been executed are skipped and the execution of the sequence diagram continues in the surrounding fragment. Figure 6.12 shows an example of this. A student wants to register for an exam. If there are no longer any places available for

Application of the seq fragments in conjunction with a break fragment

the desired date, the student makes a reservation for the next date (break fragment). In this case, the student is not examined by the lecturer and the execution of the sequence diagram continues outside the seq fragment. Irrespective of whether the registration was successful or not, the lecturer sends the message info() to the student.

Note that seq is the default order and usually does not have to be modeled explicitly. But in this case, without the explicit modeling of the seq fragment, the execution would have ended after the break fragment if incorrect password was true. This is due to the fact that after executing the content of a break fragment, the operations of the surrounding fragment are omitted. Without using seq, the surrounding fragment would have been the outermost structure of the diagram and thus the whole execution would have ended.

Figure 6.12
Example of a *seq* fragment

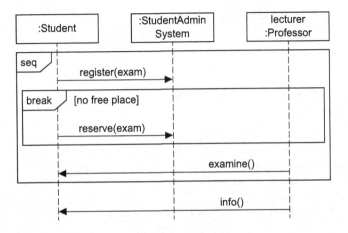

Figure 6.13 shows another sequence diagram together with all possible traces. As this diagram shows a weak order, the message c is not connected chronologically to messages a and b and can be interleaved with these messages. As b is sent by interaction partner B and d is also received by B, there is a chronological order between these two messages. In any case, e is the last message.

strict fragment

Sequential interaction with a strict order

The strict fragment describes a sequential interaction with a strict order. The order of event occurrences on different lifelines between different operands is significant, meaning that even if there is no message exchange between the interaction partners, messages in an operand that is higher up on the vertical axis are always exchanged before the messages in an operand that is lower down on the vertical axis.

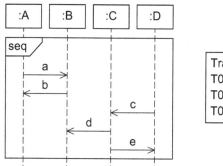

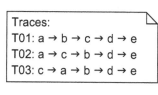

Figure 6.13
Traces in a seq fragment

In the example in Figure 6.14, a lecturer only prints an exam when a student has registered for it. If the strict fragment were not specified, it would also be possible for the lecturer to print the exam before a student registers.

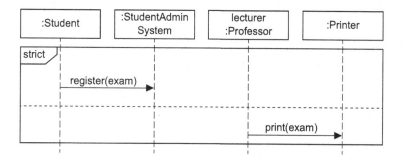

Figure 6.14
Example of a strict fragment

Figure 6.15 contains the same message sequence as Figure 6.13 but this time based on a strict order. This means that the messages are in a fixed order and there is only one trace.

The par fragment enables you to set aside any chronological order between messages in different operands. From a time perspective, the execution paths of the different operands can be interleaved as long as the restrictions of each individual operand are respected. Hence, the order of the different operands is irrelevant. However, this construct does not induce true parallelism, that is, it does not require simultaneous processing of the operands. This is contrary to what we would expect from the keyword "par" in par operators. Indeed, the par operator actually expresses *concurrency*, that is, the order of the events that are located in different operands is irrelevant. The par operator therefore has at least two operands. However, the order within an operand must be respected, meaning that there are local time axes for each operand and these must

par fragment

Concurrent interaction

Figure 6.15
Traces in a strict fragment

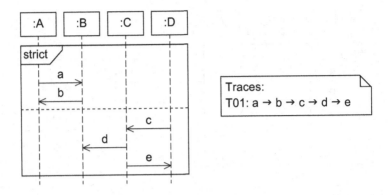

Figure 6.15
Traces in a strict fragment

be adhered to. Figure 6.16 illustrates the use of par. At the beginning
of a course, the lecturer has to complete certain activities. The lecturer
must answer queries from students, announce exam dates, and reserve
lecture halls. To do all of this, the lecturer has to communicate with different persons and systems. A par fragment is used to express that the
order in which these activities are completed is irrelevant. What is important is that the default order between messages within an operand is
adhered to, meaning that according to this sequence diagram, a student
will never register for a course first and then send a query to the lecturer.

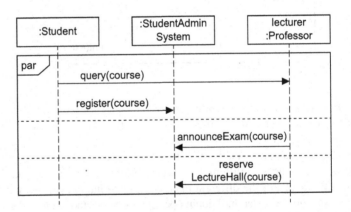

Figure 6.16
Example of a par fragment

Figure 6.17 shows the possible traces for a concurrent interaction,
whereby again the same message sequence as shown in Figure 6.13 and
Figure 6.15 is used but this time with a par fragment. There is no longer
any chronological connection between the messages from the different
operands, which explains the multitude of possible traces. What is important is that the order of the messages within an operand is respected.
For example, message a must always come before message b.

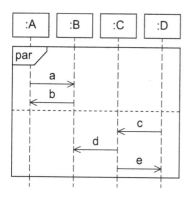

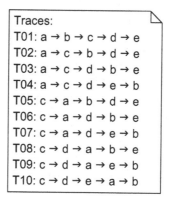

Traces:

T01: a → b → c → d → e
T02: a → c → b → d → e
T03: a → c → d → b → e
T04: a → c → d → e → b
T05: c → a → b → d → e
T06: c → a → d → b → e
T07: c → a → d → e → b
T08: c → d → a → b → e
T09: c → d → a → e → b
T10: c → d → e → a → b

Figure 6.17
Traces in a *par* fragment

Alternatively, you can set aside the chronological order of events on a single lifeline using a *coregion*. This enables you to model concurrent events for a single lifeline. The order of event occurrences within a coregion is in no way restricted, even though they are arranged along the lifeline. The area of the lifeline to be covered by the coregion is marked by square brackets rotated by 90 degrees.

Coregion

A coregion can of course contain further combined fragments executed as a whole in any order. At the corresponding points, the revocation of the chronological order spreads out to the corresponding interaction partners of the lifeline with the coregion. The example modeled in Figure 6.16 with a par fragment is modeled in Figure 6.18 with a coregion. Semantically there is no difference between these two diagrams, meaning that no chronological order is defined for the messages that the lecturer sends and receives.

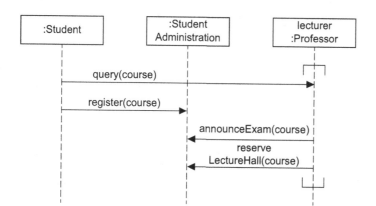

Figure 6.18
Example of the use of a coregion

critical fragment

Atomic interaction

To make sure that certain parts of an interaction are not interrupted by unexpected events, you can use the critical fragment. This marks an atomic area in the interaction. Note that the standard order seq applies within a critical fragment. We can see an example of this in Figure 6.19. The messages getExamDate and register are located in a critical fragment. This ensures that in the time between the request for an exam date and the actual registration, no message can occur that reserves the place shown as free for someone else. If the critical fragment was not present, the lecturer could execute another registration in the time between the request for free places and the registration by a student, thus taking the place away from the student.

Figure 6.19
Example of a critical fragment

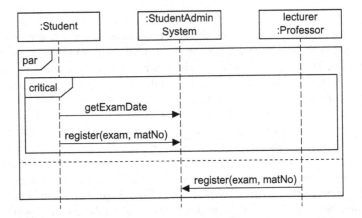

Figure 6.20 is different to Figure 6.17 only in the fact that messages c and d are enclosed by a critical fragment. This means that only those traces are valid in which message d immediately follows message c.

Figure 6.20
Traces in a critical fragment

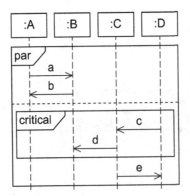

6.4.3 Filters and Assertions

Typically, a sequence diagram does not describe all aspects of an interaction. Some sequences are highlighted and explicitly declared as permitted traces. In most cases, however, there are further, permitted but
not described traces that may occur. In some cases, you have to document all possible traces that may occur or document those that must
not occur. In short, a sequence diagram contains valid, invalid, and unspecified traces. The combined fragments from the group "filters and
assertions" define (i) which messages may occur but are not relevant for
the description of the system, (ii) which messages must occur, and (iii)
which messages must not occur. Unfortunately, the description of the
fragments in this group is very compact in the UML standard, which is
why in many situations, numerous questions about their exact meaning
remain unanswered. Below we give a short breakdown of these fragments, basing our explanation as closely as possible on the standard.

Irrelevant messages are indicated by the ignore fragment, which ex-   *ignore fragment*
presses that these messages can occur at runtime but have no further   *Irrelevant interaction*
significance for the functions depicted in the model. The irrelevant
messages are noted in curly brackets after the keyword ignore. In Figure 6.21(a), the message status is contained in the set of irrelevant messages. It is used only to implement the server-client communication and
is irrelevant for the presentation of the actual functionality.

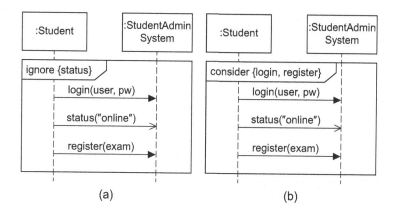

Figure 6.21
Examples of an ignore
fragment and a consider
fragment

(a)   (b)

In contrast, the consider fragment specifies those messages that are   *consider fragment*
of particular importance for the interaction under consideration. These   *Relevant interaction*
messages are also shown in set notation after the keyword. All messages
that occur in the consider fragment but that are not specified in the set of
relevant messages are automatically classified as irrelevant. They must

be treated as if they were listed as arguments of an ignore fragment (see Fig. 6.21(b), which is equivalent to Fig. 6.21(a)).

assert fragment
Asserted interaction

The assert fragment identifies certain modeled traces as mandatory. Deviations that occur in reality but that are not included in the diagram are not permitted. In effect, this means that the implementation requires precise modeling and the model is a complete specification. Figure 6.22(a) contains a corresponding example. When a student registers for an exam in the student administration system, the student receives an e-mail after the registration. If this sequence is not implemented precisely as specified, an error occurs.

neg fragment
Invalid interaction

With the neg fragment you model an invalid interaction, that is, you describe situations that must not occur. The neg fragment consists of exactly one operand. You can use this fragment to explicitly highlight frequently occurring errors and to depict critical, incorrect sequences. However, there is no limit to the number of possible interaction sequences that should/must not occur, and so you must not assume that using the neg fragment will cover all undesirable situations. Figure 6.22(b) expresses that a student may never register for an exam directly with the lecturer.

Figure 6.22
Examples of an assert
fragment and a neg
fragment

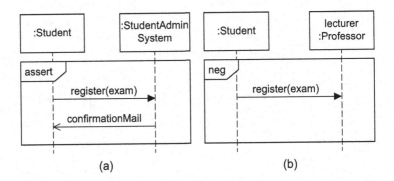

(a)   (b)

6.5 Further Language Elements

To enable us to specify interactions more precisely and to depict them more clearly, the sequence diagram offers the following additional language elements described in detail below. *Interaction references* and *continuation markers* enable you to break down sequence diagrams into modules to structure them more clearly. *Gates* allow you to model the flow of messages that takes place between different sequence diagrams or combined fragments. *Parameters* and *local attributes* specify those values required for the execution of an interaction. *Time constraints* define when certain events must occur and *state invariants* specify conditions that are necessary for the execution of the interaction.

6.5.1 Interaction References

An *interaction reference* allows you to integrate one sequence diagram in another sequence diagram. On the one hand, this allows you to reuse interactions that you have already modeled, and on the other hand, it enables you to break down complex interaction sequences into modules and to depict them in simple form. Just like a combined fragment, an interaction reference is depicted in a rectangle with a pentagon in the upper left corner. The pentagon contains the keyword ref. The rectan-

Interaction reference

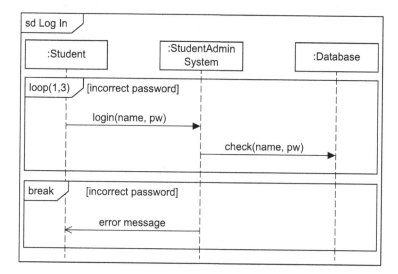

Figure 6.23
Example of an interaction reference

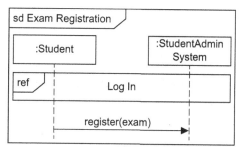

gle itself contains the name of the sequence diagram to be referenced, followed by optional arguments enclosed within parentheses, and an optional return value preceded by a colon. Figure 6.23 illustrates the use of an interaction reference. The sequence for logging in to the student administration system is modeled in the sequence diagram Log In, which is referenced in the sequence diagram Exam Registration.

6.5.2 Gates

In principle, messages must not extend beyond the boundaries of an interaction, a referenced interaction, or a combined fragment, meaning that they must not exceed the frame arbitrarily. To enable you to ex-

Gate   tend the exchange of messages beyond such boundaries, UML offers *gates*. Using such gates thus allows you to send and receive messages beyond the boundaries of the interaction fragment. A gate is visualized by the tip or the end of a message arrow—depending on whether the

Figure 6.24
Example of a gate

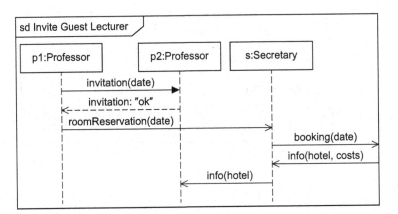

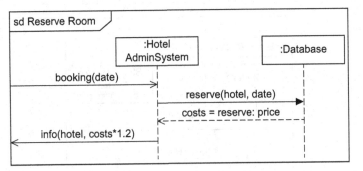

message is an incoming or outgoing message—touching the boundary of the frame that represents the sequence diagram, the interaction reference, or the combined fragment. Gates are identified either by a name or by the name of a message that uses the gate, optionally together with the direction of the message (e.g., booking in Fig. 6.24). They allow you to define a specific sender and specific receiver for each message, even if the sender or receiver is outside the respective interaction or outside the fragment. You do not have to include gates explicitly for combined fragments, meaning that a message may point directly to the receiver.

6.5.3 Continuation Markers

Continuation markers allow you to modularize the operands of an alt fragment. This enables you to break down complex interactions into parts and connect them to one another with markers. Here, a *start marker* at the end of an interaction part points to a *target marker* with the same name at the beginning of another external interaction part. Continuation markers are denoted within rectangles with rounded corners that can extend across multiple interaction partners. Continuation markers with the same name must refer to the same interaction partners. Figure 6.25 and Figure 6.26 model the example from Figure 6.10 on page 117 with three different start markers (Fig. 6.25) and the respective corresponding target markers (Fig. 6.26). If, for example, the start marker OK in Figure 6.25 is reached, the sequence diagram continues with the interactions detailed under the target marker with the same name in Figure 6.26. There is no return to the start marker—in contrast to an interaction reference, which can be compared to a macro. A continuation marker can also be the only element of an operand, thus increasing the clarity of the diagram. You can assign multiple start markers to one target marker. The target and start markers do not have to be located in the same sequence diagram.

Continuation marker

Start marker and target marker

6.5.4 Parameters and Local Attributes

Just like all of the other types of diagrams in UML 2.4.1, the sequence diagram is enclosed by a rectangular frame with a small pentagon in the upper left corner. This pentagon contains the keyword sd to clearly indicate that the content of the rectangle is a sequence diagram. The keyword sd is followed by the name of the sequence diagram and optional *parameters* separated by commas and enclosed within parentheses. You

Figure 6.25
Example of a continuation
marker (start markers)

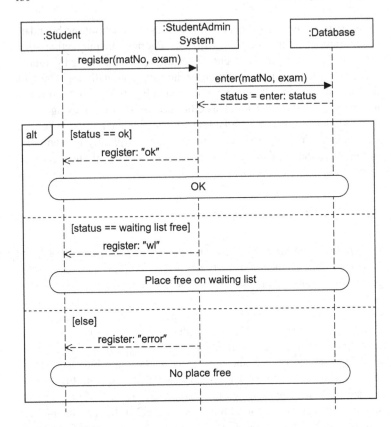

can declare *local attributes* at any point in the diagram, whereby the
syntax of the attributes corresponds to the attribute specifications in the
class diagram (see Fig. 4.5 on page 54). Alternatively, you can declare
local attributes in a note.

6.5.5 Time Constraints

Time constraint   *Time constraints* specify either the time at which events occur or a time
period between two events. Time constraints are noted in curly brackets.
Timing expression   The *timing expression* represents either a concrete time specification,
for example, {12:00}, or a calculation rule, such as {12:00+d}. You can
specify *absolute times* with the keyword at, for example, {at(12:00)}.
Relative times are specified with reference to a starting event using the
keyword after, for example, {after(5sec)}. In both cases, the timing expression is denoted within curly brackets.

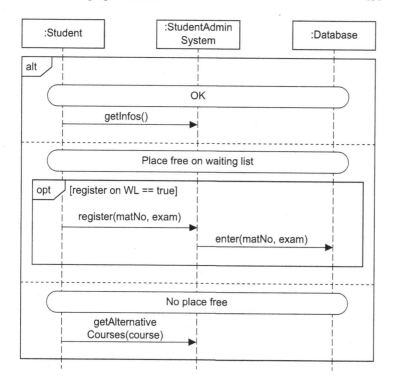

Figure 6.26
Example of a continuation
marker (target markers)

You can also specify time intervals. Again, an interval is enclosed by   *Interval*
curly brackets and contains an expression in the form lower limit..upper
limit. To express that an event takes place between 12:00 and 13:00, for
example, you would use the form {12:00..13:00}.

The keyword now specifies the current time. It can be assigned to any
attribute, for example, t=now. Naturally, you can use this attribute in any
time constraints, for example, {t..t+5}.

The calculation of the duration of a message transmission is indicated by the keyword duration.

You assign a time constraint to an event using a *timing mark* rep-   *Timing mark*
resented by a short horizontal line in the diagram. If a time constraint
refers to two events, meaning that the duration between two events is to
be defined, you specify this using two timing marks. Figure 6.27 shows
some examples of time constraints. The diagram involves communication between students and lecturers via a forum. The forum sends a
newsletter to the students at 12:00. At time t, a student posts a message
m1. Five time units later, the student receives notification that the message is being posted. A maximum of two hours later, the response from
the lecturer arrives.

Figure 6.27
Examples of time
constraints

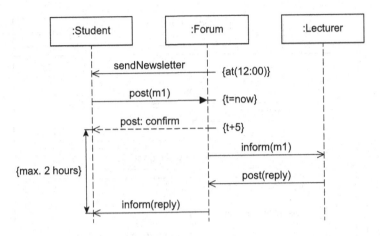

6.5.6 State Invariants

State invariant — You can specify *state invariants* for an interaction. A state invariant asserts a certain condition must be fulfilled at a certain time. It is always assigned to a specific lifeline. The evaluation of whether the invariant is true takes place before the subsequent event occurs. If the state invariant is not true, either the model or the implementation is incorrect. State invariants can reference states from the related state machine diagram or they can be logical conditions that refer to local attributes.

UML offers three notation alternatives for state invariants: you can specify a state invariant within curly brackets directly on a lifeline; you can attach it as a note; or you can also place it in a rectangle with rounded edges at the corresponding point of the lifeline. The three notation alternatives are shown in Figure 6.28. A student can only register for an exam (i) if the student is enrolled, (ii) if the exam has not yet taken place, and (iii) if registration for the exam is possible.

Figure 6.28
Notation alternatives for
state invariants

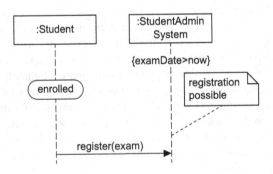

6.6 Creating a Sequence Diagram

Instead of a final example, in this section we will look at two scenarios that you can use a sequence diagram for. In particular, we will illustrate the connection between the class diagram and the sequence diagram. Then we will conclude the section with a typical application for sequence diagrams, namely the description of design patterns [20].

6.6.1 The Connection between a Class Diagram and a Sequence Diagram

We have repeatedly stated that the different UML diagrams should not be considered independently of one another; they merely offer different views of a certain content. For example, the class diagram shown in Figure 6.29 models a part of a university system that also includes the student administration system.

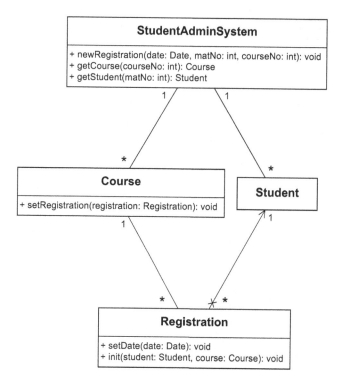

Figure 6.29
Class diagram

The student administration system has direct access to all students and courses. The system knows the registration data for students and courses that is stored in the class Registration.

We want to depict the communication that is required to create a new registration of a certain student for a certain course. To do this, the method newRegistration of the class StudentAdminSystem must be called. To create a new registration, we have to know the student object that belongs to the respective matriculation number and the course object that belongs to the given course number. We can obtain these by calling the operations getCourse and getStudent. As soon as we have this information, we can create a new object of the type Registration and call the init operation that sets the student and the course for the registration object. Now we just have to establish the connection between the registration and the course, as navigability in both directions is assumed. We do this by calling the method setRegistration. We do not have to do this for the registration and student objects, as navigation from Student to Registration is not possible. The resulting sequence diagram is shown in Figure 6.30.

Figure 6.30
Sequence diagram based on class diagram

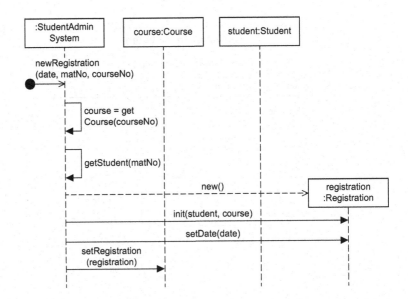

6.6.2 Describing Design Patterns

Sequence diagrams are often used to describe design patterns. Design patterns offer solutions for describing recurring problems. In the following we will look at the Transfer Object Assembler pattern [18], which describes what happens when a client in a distributed environment requires information from three business objects.

Modeling the communication of the Transfer Object Assembler pattern

In the solution shown in Figure 6.31, the client requires knowledge about the three business objects in order to access the required data. The client is therefore strongly linked to the business objects—which is generally not desirable. We can use the Transfer Object Assembler pattern to break down these dependencies. In this pattern, an assembler merges the data from multiple business objects into one transfer object that is then transferred to the client. The client thus receives the required data in an encapsulated form. In concrete terms, the pattern is implemented as described below (see Fig. 6.32).

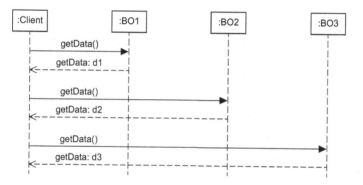

Figure 6.31
Application scenario for Transfer Object Assembler pattern

Using getData() the client requests the required information from an object of type TransferObjectAssembler (TOA). The TOA object creates the object d of type DataTransferObject (DTO) and fills it with the data from the three different business objects (BO1, BO2, BO3). The data of a business object can be queried using getData(). The object d offers setData methods that allow the entry of data. Finally, the object of type TransferObjectAssembler returns d to the client.

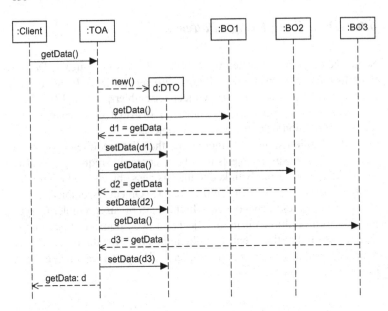

6.7 The Communication, Timing, and Interaction Overview Diagrams

In addition to the sequence diagram, UML supports three further types of interaction diagrams:

- Communication diagram
- Timing diagram
- Interaction overview diagram

The four types of interaction diagrams of UML are generally equivalent for simple interactions as they are based on the same basic elements. With the specification of the communication partners involved and the messages exchanged, they all describe certain communication situations. However, the focus is different for each type of diagram.

In this section, we briefly compare the four interaction diagrams in examples. The examples are illustrated in Figures 6.33 to 6.36, showing various aspects of the communication between a student and the e-learning system of a university.

Figure 6.33 shows the log-in process as a sequence diagram. There are three interaction partners: student, e-learning system, and database. The student wants to log in to the system and therefore sends a corresponding message to the e-learning system. A query to the database verifies the access rights and the student receives a positive response

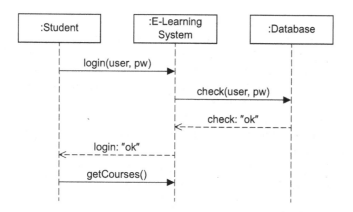

Figure 6.33
Example of sequence
diagram

message. Any possible error cases are not considered. The student then
requests the list of subscribed courses.

The *communication diagram* is a structured diagram that models the
relationships between communication partners. It therefore shows directly who communicates with whom. The relationships are the result
of the exchange of messages. Here, time is not a separate dimension.
The order in which the messages are exchanged is expressed using dec-
imal classification (sequential numbering) for the messages. Figure 6.34
shows the log-in process as a communication diagram. Again, the interaction partners are student, e-learning system, and database. The diagram shows that the student communicates with the e-learning system
twice: once using login(user, pw) and once using getCourses(). It also
shows that the e-learning system communicates with the database using
check(user, pw). The numbering results in the order login, check, and get-
Courses. All three messages are synchronous messages, as shown by the
arrowheads; asynchronous messages would be shown with open arrowheads as in a sequence diagram. Response messages are not depicted in
the communication diagram.

Communication diagram

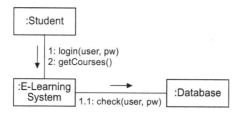

Figure 6.34
Example of communica-
tion diagram

Timing diagram   The *timing diagram* shows state changes of the interaction partners
that result from the occurrence of events. In contrast to the sequence
diagram, in which the arrangement of the interaction partners and the
time axis is exactly the opposite, in the timing diagram the interaction
partners are listed on the vertical axis and the horizontal axis represents
the chronological order. In the timing diagram, lifelines are depicted by
a whole area in which states and state transitions can be represented.
The name of the lifeline (role name and/or class) is noted vertically at
the left boundary of the area. Figure 6.35 thus shows the interaction
partners student, e-learning system, and database. A student can be in
the state logged in or logged out and the e-learning system can take the
states idle or busy. For the database there is only the state active. If the
student now sends the message login(user, pw) to the e-learning system,
the system changes from the state idle to the state busy and sends the
message check(user,pw) to the database. The database verifies the data
and thus the student is allowed access to the system. The student is
informed of this with a corresponding response message. The student is
now in the state logged in. The e-learning system can briefly return to
the state idle until the student sends the getCourses request.

Figure 6.35
Example of timing diagram

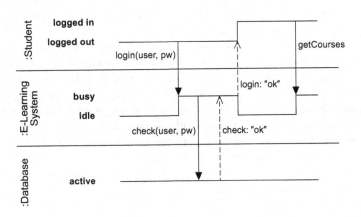

Interaction overview   The *interaction overview diagram* shows the different interactions
diagram   and visualizes the order in and conditions under which they take place.
This allows you to place various interaction diagrams in a logical order. To do this, you use primarily the concepts of the activity diagram
(see Chapter 7). Instead of specifying nodes for actions and objects, you
specify entire interaction diagrams and interaction references as nodes
which you can then place in order using the control structures of the
activity diagram. A solid circle represents the initial node and a solid
circle with a surrounding circle represents a final node. You can implement different paths using decision nodes represented by a hollow

diamond. Figure 6.36 shows an interaction overview diagram that, in addition to an initial and final node, also contains this type of branch node. If the student has the necessary authorization, the student can execute the interaction Forum, represented as a sequence diagram.

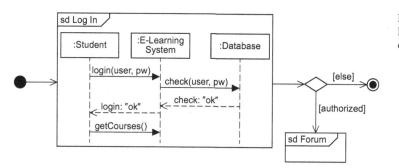

Figure 6.36
Example of interaction overview diagram

6.8 Summary

The sequence diagram is one of four interaction diagrams in UML. Interaction diagrams model the communication between different interaction partners, whereby each of the four diagrams focuses on a different aspect. In practice, the sequence diagram is the most frequently used of the interaction diagrams. The presentation of communication protocols and design patterns are particularly prominent applications of sequence diagrams as they enable a compact and clear specification. In addition to the interaction partners, which are depicted in the form of lifelines, the sequence diagram contains different types of messages (synchronous, asynchronous, response message, create message). The chronological order of the messages is generally assumed to be from top to bottom along the vertical line. Twelve types of combined fragments provide you with different control structures that enable you to control the interaction. The most important elements of the sequence diagram are summarized in Table 6.2.

Table 6.2
Notation elements for the
sequence diagram

Name	Notation	Description
Lifeline	r:C A	Interaction partners involved in the communication
Destruction event		Time at which an interaction partner ceases to exist
Combined fragment	... [...]	Control constructs
Synchronous message		Sender waits for a response message
Response message		Response to a synchronous message
Asynchronous message		Sender continues its own work after sending the asynchronous message
Lost message	lost	Message to an unknown receiver
Found message	found	Message from an unknown sender

Chapter 7
The Activity Diagram

The *activity diagram* focuses on modeling procedural processing aspects of a system. It specifies the control flow and data flow between various steps—the *actions*—required to implement an activity.

Control flow and data flow

In UML 2, activity diagrams use flow-oriented language concepts that find their origins in languages for defining business processes. Activity diagrams are also based on established concepts for describing concurrent communicating processes, such as the token concept of Petri nets [41]. One particular feature of activity diagrams is their support for modeling both object-oriented systems and non-object-oriented systems. They allow you to define activities independently of objects, which means, for example, that you can model function libraries as well as business processes and real-world organizations.

Modeling of object-oriented and non-object-oriented systems

The UML standard does not stipulate any specific form of notation for activities. In addition to the flow-based notation elements of the activity diagrams, the standard also allows other forms of notation, such as structural diagrams or even pseudocode. A number of recurring control flow and data flow patterns have emerged in addition to custom notation elements. They are used in particular for modeling business processes and have proven to be very useful for complex processes. These constructs are referred to as "workflow patterns". For an overview of these types of patterns as well as guidance on how to model the patterns based on the concepts of UML 2 activity diagrams, see Wohed et al. [44].

"Workflow patterns"

In this chapter, observant readers will note that not all examples model complete processes—some of the models are restricted to extracts of processes. Thus, for example, some of the diagrams do not contain initial and final nodes. In practice, however, a complete activity diagram must have clearly defined start and end points.

© Springer International Publishing Switzerland 2015
M. Seidl et al., *UML @ Classroom*, Undergraduate Topics
in Computer Science, DOI 10.1007/978-3-319-12742-2_7

7.1 Activities

Activity

An activity diagram allows you to specify user-defined behavior in the form of activities. An *activity* itself can describe the implementation of a use case. At a very detailed level, it can also define the behavior of an operation in the form of individual instructions, or at a less detailed level, model the functions of a business process. A business process defines how business partners have to interact with one another to achieve their goals. It can also describe the internal processes within a company. Behavior can thus be defined at different levels of granularity. An activity can be assigned to an operation of a class but it can also be autonomous.

Activity

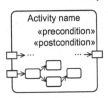

The content of an activity is—as with Petri nets—a directed graph whose nodes represent the components of the activity like actions, data stores, and control elements and whose edges represent the control flow or object flow, that is, the possible execution paths for the activity.

An activity is depicted as a rectangle with rounded corners and can, just like an operation, have *parameters*. These are shown as rectangles arranged overlapping at the boundary of the activity. To make the diagram easier to read, you should position *input parameters* at the left or upper boundary and *output parameters* at the right or lower boundary of the activity. This allows an activity to be read from left to right and/or from top to bottom. The values that are transferred to the activity via the input parameters are available to those actions that are connected to the input parameters by a directed edge (see the next section). In the same way, output parameters receive their values via directed edges from actions within the activity. The example in Figure 7.1 shows the steps necessary to execute the activity Take exam. The input parameters are the matriculation number and the study program ID of a student. The actions Register, Write exam, and Correct are executed in this activity. The result of the activity is a grade. This example diagram does not show, however, who performs which action. To enable actions to be assigned to specific actors, the activity diagram offers the concept of partitions, which we will introduce in Section 7.5.

Precondition and postcondition

You can specify preconditions and postconditions for an activity. These indicate which conditions have to be fulfilled before or after the activity is executed. The keywords «precondition» and «postcondition» are used to identify the respective conditions. In Figure 7.1, a student who wants to take an exam must be enrolled. After the activity Take exam has been executed, the student must be graded.

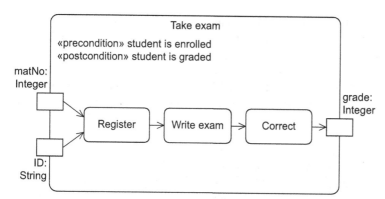

Figure 7.1
Example of an activity

7.2 Actions

The basic elements of activities are *actions*. Just like an activity, an action is depicted as a rectangle with rounded corners, whereby the name of the action is positioned centrally within the rounded rectangle. You can use actions to specify any user-defined behavior. There are no specific language requirements for the description of an action. Therefore, you can define the actions in natural language or in any programming language. For example, if, as a result of the execution of an action, the value of the variable i is to be increased by one, you can express this by using i++ or simply by writing Increase i by one.

Action

> Action

Actions process input values to produce output values, which means that they are able to perform calculations. They can also load data from a memory and they can change the current state of a system. In the example in Figure 7.1, Register, Write exam, and Correct are actions.

Within the context of an activity, actions are always atomic—that is, they cannot be broken down further within the modeled context. However, an action can refer to another activity that itself consists of actions (see call behavior action on page 145). Actions are considered atomic, even though they might consist of multiple individual steps. For example, registering for an exam usually requires multiple steps such as logging on to the system and selecting the appropriate course and the exam date. Despite this, in Figure 7.1, we have intentionally modeled Register as an action rather than an activity. This is because in the present model, the execution of a registration is considered as a single step; the internal details of this step are of no interest to us, however, and therefore we do not break it down further.

Atomicity of actions

As we can see in Figure 7.1, actions and parameters are connected to one another via directed edges. These edges express the order in which the actions are executed and thus define the execution steps of

Edge between actions

an activity. Here we differentiate between *control flow edges* and *object flow edges*: control flow edges only define the order between actions, whereas object flow edges can also be used to exchange data or objects. This enables you to express a data dependency between a preceding action and a subsequent action. The completion of an action can initiate the execution of another action if these two actions are connected with one another via control flow edges or object flow edges. However, an action may only be executed if all previous actions have been completed successfully, all relevant guards evaluate to true and all input parameters have values. Guards are conditions that must be fulfilled to enable the transition from one activity or action to another activity or action. They usually occur in connection with alternative branches. We will look at the control flow, including the guards, and the object flow more closely in the following two sections after we have introduced two special types of actions.

Control flow edge versus object flow edge

Predefined actions

In UML, there are a number of predefined, non-language-specific actions that you can model easily in any target language due to their level of detail.

The predefined actions in UML can be classified into different categories based on their function and complexity. We will discuss the most important two of these categories in the following sections.

7.2.1 Event-Based Actions

Accept (time) event action

Event-based actions enable objects and signals to be transmitted to receiver objects. They allow you to distinguish between different types of events. You can use an *accept event action* to model an action that waits for the occurrence of a specific event. The notation element for an accept event action is a "concave pentagon"—a rectangle with a tip that points inwards from the left. If the event is a time-based event, you can use an *accept time event action*, whereby in this case, the notation is an hourglass.

Accept (time) event actions do not necessarily have incoming edges. If they do not have incoming edges, they start when the corresponding event occurs. They remain active, that is, they can receive signals until the activity that contains them is ended. Figure 7.2 shows three examples of accept (time) event actions: whenever a fire alarm is triggered, the lecture hall must be evacuated (Fig. 7.2(a)); at the end of a semester, certificates are issued (Fig. 7.2(b)); when a student has taken an exam, the student waits for the grade and inspects the exam paper when receiving the grade (Fig. 7.2(c)).

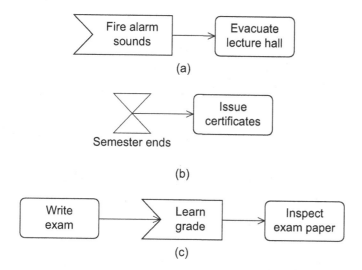

Figure 7.2
Examples of accept event
actions (a+c) and accept
time event actions (b)

To send signals, you can use *send signal actions*. Send signal actions are denoted with a "convex pentagon"—a rectangle with a tip that protrudes to the right. The action Send grade in Figure 7.3(b) is an example of a send signal action.

Send signal action

7.2.2 Call Behavior Actions

Actions can call activities themselves. These actions are referred to as *call behavior actions* and are marked with an inverted fork symbol. This fork symbol indicates a hierarchy. It symbolizes that the execution of this action starts another activity, thus dividing the system into various parts. Figure 7.3(a) shows an example of a call behavior action. In this diagram, the action Issue certificate in the activity Organize exam refers to an activity that specifies Issue certificate in more detail. Within the context of the activity Organize exam, the internal steps that lead to the issue of a certificate are not relevant. Therefore, Issue certificate is seen as an atomic unit here, even though it involves a process with multiple actions.

Call behavior action

The content of the called activity can be depicted elsewhere in this or even another activity diagram in the form of an activity with the usual notation for activities that we have already seen. Figure 7.3(b) shows the details of the called activity Issue certificate with the input parameter grade.

Figure 7.3
Example of a call behavior
action and a send signal
action

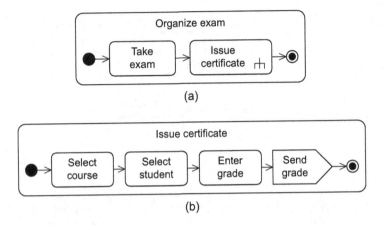

(a)

(b)

Call operation action

An action can also trigger the call of an operation. This type of action is referred to as a *call operation action*. It is represented in a rectangle with rounded edges. If the name of the operation does not match the name of the action, the name of the operation can be specified beneath the name of the action in the form (ClassName::operationName).

7.3 Control Flows

Token for describing flows

Activities consist of other activities and actions that are connected to one another by edges. If we look at the graph of an activity, the static structure does not show clearly how the execution works. To integrate the dynamic behavior aspects into the diagram, we need execution semantics, meaning that we have to specify exactly how an activity diagram is executed.

Token flow

The token concept, as introduced in Petri nets [41], is the basis for the execution semantics of the activity diagram. A token is a virtual coordination mechanism that describes the execution exactly. In this context, virtual means that the tokens are not physical components of the diagram. They are mechanisms that grant actions an execution permission.

If an action receives a token, the action is active and can be executed. Once the action has ended, it passes the token to a subsequent node via an edge and thus triggers the execution of this action. Once this action has ended, it passes the token to the outgoing edges or retains it until a certain condition is fulfilled.

Guard

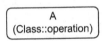

The passing of a token can be prevented by a *guard* evaluating to false. A guard is specified in square brackets. In the example in Figure 7.4, an exam is only held if students have registered for it.

Figure 7.4
Example of a guard

An action can only be executed if tokens are present at all of its incoming edges. If an action has multiple outgoing edges, a token is offered to all target nodes of these edges, thereby causing a split into multiple independent execution paths. Special nodes are also available as an alternative for modeling this concurrency. We will look at these in more detail later on.

When an action is executed, usually one token of each of its incoming edges is consumed. Alternatively, a *weight* may be placed on an edge to allow a certain number of tokens to be consumed at that edge by a single execution. The weight of an edge is specified in curly brackets with the keyword weight. It is always a whole number greater than or equal to zero. If the weight is zero, this means that all tokens present are consumed. Alternatively, all or ∗ can also be written instead of zero. If no weight is specified, 1 is assumed as the default value. Figure 7.5 gives an example of the use of weights. If the signal Register is received 30 times, meaning that at least 30 students have registered and thus 30 tokens are offered to the subsequent action, then this subsequent action is executed, consumes 30 tokens, and a new group is created.

Weight of an edge

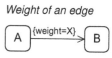

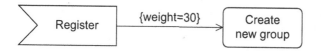

Figure 7.5
Example of the weight of an edge

If two actions that are to be connected to one another via an edge are far apart in a diagram, you can use *connectors* to make the diagram clearer. In this case, you do not have to draw the edge as a continuous line from one action to the other; instead, the connector acts as a continuation marker comparable to the continuation markers in sequence diagrams (see page 129). A connector is depicted as a small circle containing the name of the connector. Each connector must appear twice in an activity: once with an incoming edge and once with an outgoing edge. Figure 7.6 models a relationship between two actions, once without a connector (Fig. 7.6(a)) and once with a connector (Fig. 7.6(b)).

Connector

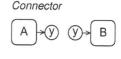

The activity diagram offers special nodes for controlling the control flow. These nodes are called *control nodes*.

The *initial node* indicates where the execution of an activity begins. It does not have any incoming edges but has at least one outgoing edge and is noted as a solid black circle. As soon as an activity becomes

Initial node

Figure 7.6
Example of a connector

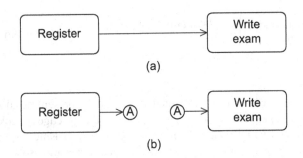

(a)

(b)

active, tokens are provided at all outgoing edges of an initial node and thus the activity is started. Figure 7.7 shows an example of an initial node. The diagram also contains an activity final node that represents the end of an activity. We will look at the activity final node, noted by a solid black circle within another circle, in more detail later in this chapter.

Figure 7.7
Example of an initial node

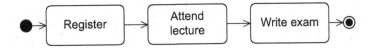

Multiple initial nodes are also permitted for each activity. This allows you to express concurrency, meaning that multiple execution paths can be active simultaneously. If an activity with multiple initial nodes is called, the outgoing edges of all initial nodes are supplied with tokens simultaneously. The example in Figure 7.8 shows two concurrent subpaths of the activity Conduct lecture. If the activity Conduct lecture is activated, a token is placed at each of the two initial nodes and thus both subpaths are activated. One subpath relates to the actions of students and the other subpath refers to the actions performed by a lecturer. In the action Write exam, both paths are merged. A token must be present at both incoming edges for the action Write exam to be executed.

Figure 7.8
Example with multiple initial nodes

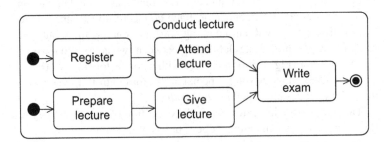

In an activity diagram, you can model alternative branches using *de-*   *Decision node*
cision nodes. These act as a switch point for tokens and correspond to
the `if` statement in a conventional programming language. A decision

node is depicted as a diamond with one incoming edge and multiple
outgoing edges. The outgoing edges have guards (also referred to as
conditions). Just like in the other UML diagrams, guards are boolean
expressions enclosed within square brackets. These conditions must not
overlap, meaning that the system must be able to clearly decide which
outgoing edge a token should take in a specific situation. For example,
having one outgoing edge with the condition [x > 1] and another outgoing edge with the condition [x < 3] is not allowed, as there would be no
unique choice of the edge a token should take if x = 2 applies. If there
is a token at a decision node, the system must be able to clearly decide,
based on the current context (for example, dependent on the value of
a variable), which path the token takes to exit the decision node. Figure 7.9 shows an example of a decision node. If the action Register is
executed, it is followed by the action Select group if there are still places
available. If this is not the case, the action Enter on waiting list is executed.

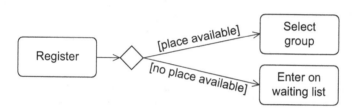

Figure 7.9
Example of a decision
node

You can specify *decision behavior* for a decision node. This means   *Decision behavior*
that you can specify behavior that is necessary for the evaluation of the
guards. It allows you to avoid situations in which the same calculations

have to be performed multiple times for different guards as the result of
the calculation can be accessed in every guard. However, this behavior
must not result in any side effects, meaning that the execution of the
behavior defined in a decision node must never change the values of
objects and variables. The decision behavior is attached to the decision
node as a comment with the label «decisionInput». Figure 7.10 shows
an example of this. As soon as the exam results are known, a decision
is taken in a central department regarding whether to offer students the
opportunity to inspect their corrected exam papers. If the decision is
positive, the students are allowed to inspect their exam papers. Their
certificates are issued afterwards. If the decision is negative, the certificates are issued immediately.

Figure 7.10
Example of decision
behavior

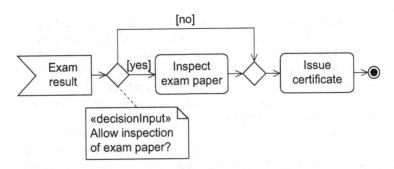

Merge node

If you want to bring alternative subpaths back together again, you can do this using the *merge node*. This node is also depicted as a diamond but with multiple incoming edges and only one outgoing edge. In particular, a token may only be present at one incoming edge at most. Using decision and merge nodes, we can now model execution steps that are repeated, that is, loops (see Fig. 7.11).

Figure 7.11
Example of a loop

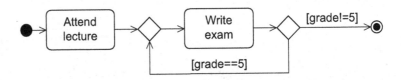

Combined decision and merge node

You can also combine decision and merge nodes. This combined node then has multiple incoming edges and multiple outgoing edges.

For decision and merge nodes, only one of the possible paths is active. As already mentioned, you can use multiple initial nodes to model concurrency at the beginning of an activity. If an execution path splits into multiple simultaneously active execution paths later on, you can realize this using a *parallelization node*. A parallelization node is depicted as a black bar with one incoming edge and multiple outgoing edges. Figure 7.12 shows an example of this type of node. Once a student has registered for a course, the student attends the lecture and participates in the assignment simultaneously. The student can only write the exam when both the lecture and the assignment have been completed (see next paragraph).

Parallelization node

Synchronization node

You can merge concurrent subpaths using a *synchronization node*. This node is the counterpart to the parallelization node. It is depicted as a black bar with multiple incoming edges but only one outgoing edge. As soon as tokens are present at all incoming edges, that is, as soon as all preceding actions have been executed, all incoming tokens are merged into one token that is passed on at the outgoing edge.

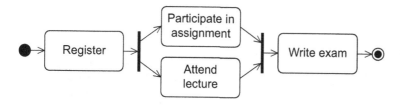

Figure 7.12
Example of the use of
parallelization and syn-
chronization nodes

In the same way that you can combine decision and merge nodes, you can also combine synchronization and parallelization nodes using a bar with multiple incoming edges and multiple outgoing edges.

Combined parallelization and synchronization node

To express the end of an activity, the activity diagram offers a special node for this purpose: the *activity final node*. This node is depicted as a small circle containing a solid circle and is often referred to as a "bull's eye". If a token is present at an incoming edge of an activity final node, the entire activity is terminated—that is, all active actions of this activity are terminated. This also includes active concurrent subpaths and thus all tokens in the activity are deleted. An exception to this rule is data tokens that are already present at the output parameters of the activity (see the next section). If a diagram contains multiple activity final nodes, the first one reached during the execution ends the entire activity. For example, participation in a course is ended if either the assignment has not been passed or the exam has been taken (see Fig. 7.13).

Activity final node

You can merge multiple activity final nodes into one activity final node with multiple incoming edges. As soon as one token reaches the activity final node via an incoming edge, the entire activity is ended.

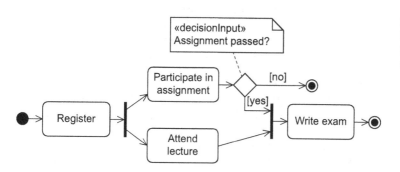

Figure 7.13
Example of multiple ac-
tivity final nodes in one
activity diagram

If you only want to end one execution path, leaving the other concurrently active execution paths unaffected, you have to use the *flow final node*. This node only deletes the tokens that flow into it directly, thus ending just the respective path. All other tokens of the activity remain unaffected and may continue to exist. The flow final node is represented by a small circle containing an X and has only incoming edges.

Flow final node

Figure 7.14
Example of a flow final
node and an activity final
node

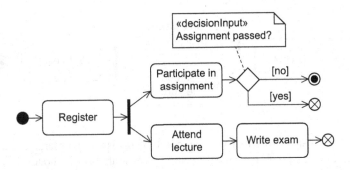

In Figure 7.14, the example from Figure 7.13 has been modified.
The successful participation in an assignment and the simultaneous at-
tendance of the related lecture combined with taking the exam are two
independent execution paths that each end with a flow final node. However, failing the assignment ends the entire activity, meaning that if a
student has a negative assignment grade, the student can no longer take
the final exam if the student has not done so already.

Using Figure 7.15, we will now demonstrate the execution semantics
of the individual control nodes applying the token concept.

If activity A is activated, all outgoing edges of all initial nodes are
assigned a token. Thus, in our example, action A1 receives a token and
starts the execution. Once A1 has been successfully completed, it passes
the token on to the decision node. Depending on the value of the variable
x, the decision node passes the token to A2 if [x ≤ 0] is true or to A3 if [x >
0] is true. The subsequent merge node passes on every token it receives
to the subsequent node. Thus, after the execution of A2 or A3, the action
A4 is activated. The subsequent parallelization node duplicates the token
for all outgoing edges, thus creating three tokens and activating A5, A6,
and A7. The following three execution paths are taken concurrently:

- One token activates A5. As soon as the execution of A5 has ended,
  the token passes to the flow final node which then ends this execution
  path. No other execution path is affected.
- A further token activates A6. After the execution of A6, all outgoing
  edges from A6 are assigned tokens and thus A8 and A9 are executed
  concurrently. A10 can only be executed when tokens are present at
  all incoming edges, that is, when A8 and A9 have been completed. If
  we look at the token flow, we can see that multiple outgoing edges of
  an action are equivalent to a parallelization node. If multiple edges
  lead into an action node, all incoming execution paths have to be
  completed before the execution of this action. This behavior could
  also be modeled using synchronization nodes as an alternative.
- The third token activates A7.

When A7 and A10 have both been successfully executed and there is thus a token at both incoming edges of the synchronization node, these tokens are merged into one token and A11 is activated. Depending on the value of the variable y, the decision node passes the token to A12 if [y ≤ 0] is true or to A13 if [y > 0] is true. In both cases, after execution of the respective activity, the token enters the activity final node. When the token reaches the activity final node, the entire activity is ended. Any remaining tokens are withdrawn from all actions. Therefore, for example, the execution of A5 is terminated if this action has not yet ended at this point in time.

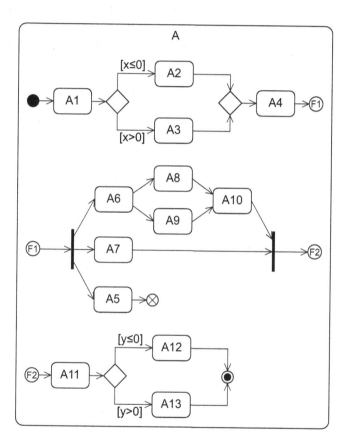

Figure 7.15
Example of the token concept

7.4 Object Flows

Control tokens vs data
tokens Up to this point, we have looked mainly at the control flow, concentrating on the logical sequence of actions. The described token concept used exclusively *control tokens*. For the purposes of simplification, we have referred to these simply as tokens so far. However, it may be the case, or is even very probable, that actions exchange data using *data tokens*. Just like control tokens, these are never drawn in the diagram and are also used only to describe the execution semantics of activity diagrams. Data tokens are implicitly also control tokens, as the exchange of these tokens influences the flow of the activity. Data can be the result of an action and can also serve as input for a subsequent action. However, data can also be received via the input parameters of the activity and passed on to output parameters, as already described above (see Fig. 7.1 on page 143).

Input parameters are usually only read once at the beginning of the activity and output parameters are written once at the end of the activity. If you want to allow the parameters to be read and written continually during the execution of the activity, you can label the input or output parameter with the keyword {stream}. Figure 7.16 shows examples of streams for input and output parameters of activities or actions (parameters for actions are described below). Streaming parameters for actions can be noted by a filled rectangle.

Figure 7.16
Example of streams

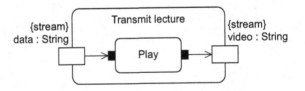

When the activity is ended, any output parameters that have no token are assigned a null token. Within an activity, you can use *object nodes* to explicitly represent the exchange of data. Object nodes can be depicted in various ways. They are shown either as a separate node as in the object diagram (see page 49) or they are attached to an action directly as input or output pins. Figure 7.17 gives an example of an object node as an independent node. It is added as a rectangle between the action that delivers the data and the action that consumes the data. The rectangle contains the name of the object that it represents. You can optionally specify an object type as well. Within square brackets, you can also stipulate the state that the object must be in.

Object nodes

Object

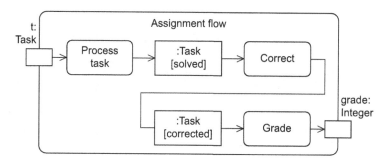

Figure 7.17
Example of an object node

The *pin notation* for actions corresponds to the notation of parameters of an activity. It is used in the same way to represent objects that serve as input and output for actions. A small rectangle is specified at the beginning or end of the edge at the boundary of the corresponding action. The pin can be annotated with the same information that we use when explicitly representing object nodes as rectangles. Figure 7.18 shows an example.

Pins

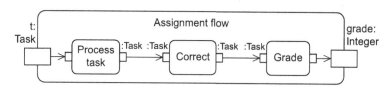

Figure 7.18
Example of an object node in pin notation

The activity diagram offers special object nodes for saving and passing on data tokens: the central buffer and the data store. The *central buffer* is a special object node that manages the data flow between multiple sources and multiple receivers. It accepts incoming data tokens from object nodes and passes these on to other object nodes. In contrast to pins and activity parameters, a central buffer is not bound to actions or activities. When a data token is read from the central buffer, it is deleted there and cannot be consumed again. Figure 7.19 shows an example of the use of a central buffer. To execute the action Grant access authorization, a key must be withdrawn from the KeyCabinet. The key is then no longer in the KeyCabinet until it is returned in the action Withdraw access authorization.

Central buffer

«centralBuffer»
CB

In a *data store*, all data tokens that flow into the data store are saved permanently, meaning that they are copied before they leave the data store again. You can define queries regarding the content of the data store at the outgoing edges leading from the data store. These queries are attached to the outgoing edge using the note symbol. A data store can therefore model the functionality of a database. Figure 7.20 shows

Data store

«datastore»
DS

Figure 7.19
Example of a central buffer

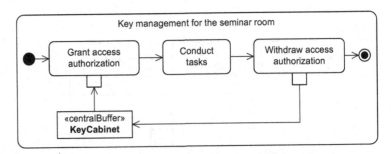

an example of the use of a data store. The performance of the partic-
ipants of a course is managed in the data store ExamData. This data
includes the assessment of assignment tasks and exam results necessary
for calculating the overall grade.

Figure 7.20
Example of a data store

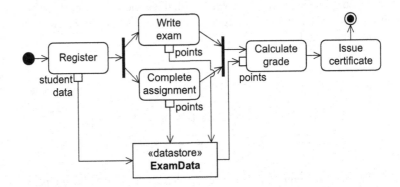

A central buffer represents transient memory, whereas a data store
represents permanent memory. With the former, the information can
only be used once, meaning that once it has been read from the central buffer and forwarded it is lost. With a data store, the information
can be used as often as required, provided it has been saved once in the
data store.

7.5 Partitions

Partition

A *partition* allows you to group nodes and edges of an activity based on
common properties. If we consider a business process, for example, we
could use a partition to group all actions that a specific entity is responsible for executing. UML has no strict rules regarding the grouping criteria that can be used. Generally, partitions reflect organizational units

or roles that are responsible for the execution of the actions within the partitions. You can specify partitions at different levels of detail down to the level of individual classes. Partitions may overlap and be nested in any way required. They do not change the meaning of the execution semantics of an activity diagram, which is defined by tokens. This means that partitions do not influence the token flow but merely represent a logical view of its components. Partitions make the diagram clearer, enabling you to see the areas of responsibility quickly, thus introducing more detailed information into the model.

Partitions can be depicted either graphically or in textual form. When depicted in graphic form, they are placed on top of the activity diagram as "open" rectangles. All elements that lie within an "open" rectangle belong to a common group. The name of the partition is specified at one end of the rectangle. Due to their appearance, partitions are also referred to as *swimlanes*. Figure 7.21 shows an example of the use of partitions in an activity diagram that models the execution of an exam. The parties involved are a student, an assistant, and a professor. The use of partitions allows each of these actors to be assigned the actions that they have to perform.

Synonyms:

- *Partition*
- *Swimlane*

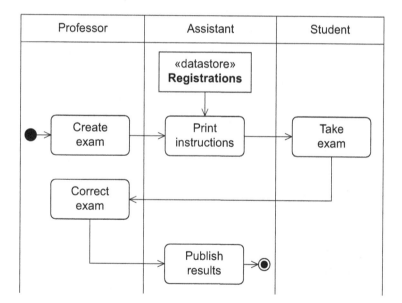

Figure 7.21
Example of one-dimensional partitions

A partition can itself be subdivided into multiple *subpartitions*. Figure 7.22 shows an example of this. In this example, the institute employees Professor and Secretary are involved in the execution of an exam.

Subpartition

Figure 7.22
Example of subpartitions

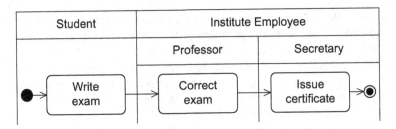

As we can see in the example in Figure 7.23, partitions can also be multi-dimensional. In this example, we model correspondence between a professor of the Johannes Kepler University Linz (JKU Linz) and the Vienna University of Technology (TU Vienna). The Professor at TU Vienna writes a letter to the Professor at JKU Linz. The professor gives the letter to the Secretary, who takes the letter to the post office. The Secretary at JKU Linz fetches the letter from the mailbox as soon as the letter arrives and has it delivered to the Professor at JKU Linz, who then reads it. This shows how we need multi-dimensional partitions when various groups of actors can appear in various forms.

Figure 7.23
Example of multi-dimensional partitions

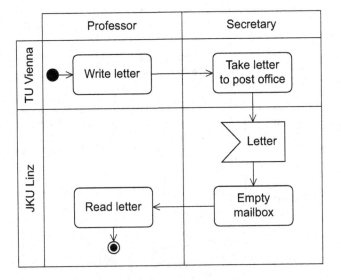

You can also assign an action to a partition or—in the case of multi-dimensional partitions—to a set of partitions in text form. In this situation, you specify the partitions in parentheses above the action name. If the action belongs to multiple partitions, these partitions are listed separated by a comma, for example (Partition 1, Partition 2). When specifying

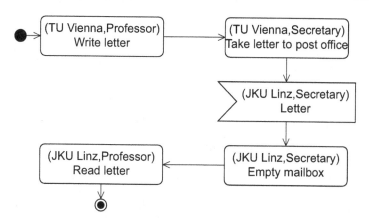

Figure 7.24
Example of multi-
dimensional partitions
with textual notation

subpartitions, you use a double colon—(Partition::Subpartition)—to express a hierarchical partitioning. The activity diagram from Figure 7.24 shows the example from Figure 7.23 in this notation.

7.6 Exception Handling

If an error occurs during the execution of an action, the execution is terminated. In this situation, there is no guarantee that the action will deliver the expected output. If an action has an *exception handler* for a specific error situation, this exception handler is activated when an exception occurs. Using an exception handler, you can define how the system is to react in a specific error situation e. This allows you to minimize the effects of this error. You specify an exception handler for a specific type of error—that is, you can use different exception handlers for different errors. If an error situation occurs, all tokens in the action concerned are deleted immediately. If there is a matching exception handler, this replaces the content of the action concerned and instead, the content of the exception handler is executed. The sequence then continues as the regular path of the activity as if the defective action had ended normally. As an exception handler is an activity node, it is depicted as a rectangle with rounded corners. The action safeguarded by the exception handler points to the exception handler with a lightning bolt arrow. The tip of the arrow is labeled with the type of the error. Figure 7.25 shows two examples for handling exceptions. If a paper jam occurs during printing, printing can continue once the paper jam has been removed. If there is no paper in the printer, paper must be inserted for printing to continue until sufficient copies of the exam instructions have been printed.

Exception handler

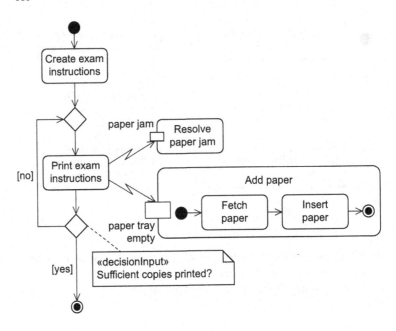

Figure 7.25
Examples of exception handling

If there are multiple matching exception handlers, the handler to be executed is not specified. If there is no matching exception handler, the exception is forwarded to the surrounding structure. If the exception is passed to the outermost activity without a matching exception handler being found, the behavior of the system is undefined.

An exception handler has no explicit incoming or outgoing edges. It has the same access rights to variables and values as the nodes that it safeguards. The tokens that result from the execution of the content of the exception handler become result tokens of the safeguarded node. Therefore, the exception handler and the safeguarded node must have the same number of return values. This ensures that in the event of an error, every outgoing edge of the safeguarded node receives the required token.

Interruptible activity region

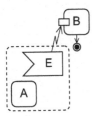

The *interruptible activity region* offers a further way to handle exceptions. Using this concept, you can define a group of actions whose execution is to be terminated immediately if a specific event occurs. The interruptible activity region is depicted as a dashed rectangle with rounded corners that encloses the relevant actions. The execution of these events is monitored for the occurrence of a specific event, for example an error. If the event does occur during this execution, then as a consequence certain behavior is executed. Within the interruptible activity region, you model an accept event action that represents the special event and leads out from the edge in lightning bolt form to an activity outside the interruptible activity region. If the modeled event occurs, all control tokens in the interruptible activity region are deleted and the action that the accept event action points to is activated. Figure 7.26 shows an example of an interruptible activity region. If a student withdraws from the university while attending a course, the action Withdraw student is executed. However, a withdrawal is only possible if the student has previously registered and if the action Take exam has not yet ended. In all other cases a certificate is issued.

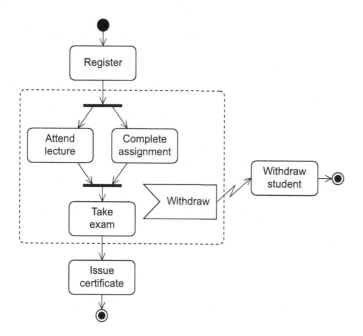

Figure 7.26
Example of an interruptible activity region

7.7 Concluding Example

To sum up, we look at the process that has to be executed for a future student of a university to receive a student identification card (student ID). We use an activity diagram to model this process. In textual form, the process of issuing a student ID can be described as follows: To obtain a student ID, the student must request this ID from an employee of the student office. The employee hands the student the forms that the student has to fill out to register at the university. These forms include the student ID itself, which is a small, old-style cardboard card. The student has to enter personal data on this card and the employee confirms it with a stamp after checking it against certain documents. The student ID is only valid if it has a current semester label. Once the student has filled out the forms, the student returns them to the employee in the student office and hands over documents such as photo identification, school-leaving certificate, and birth certificate. The employee checks the documents. If the documents are incomplete or the student is not authorized to receive a student ID for the university, the process is terminated immediately. If the documents are all in order, the employee checks whether the student has filled out the student ID correctly. If there are any errors, this ID is destroyed and the student has to fill out another one. Otherwise the ID is stamped. However, the student ID is not valid until it bears the semester label sent to the student by post.

Two actors are involved in the process to be modeled: the Student and the Employee. To assign the individual actions precisely, we use partitions. We can derive the actions and the control flow directly from the text above and these are shown in Figure 7.27. To model the termination of the process in the event of invalid or incomplete documents, we use a decision node where one path leads to an activity final node. The requirement that part of the entire process has to be repeated if the forms are filled out incorrectly results in the use of a loop. We implement this with a decision node after the action Check ID and a merge node before the action Create ID. If we were to allow the edge to lead directly to the node of the action Create ID, we would need two tokens for the execution of this action. As this will never happen, it is important to use a merge node. If the student has handed over the documents completely and filled out the forms correctly, the student ID is stamped and the student receives the current semester label by post. We model this action as an accept event action. To validate the ID, the student must then affix the label. This action ends the process that has to be executed to obtain a new student ID.

In the activity diagram in Figure 7.27, we have modeled only the control flow. However, in this example, an object is changed: the student ID. Initially it is blank, then filled out, then stamped. A student ID is not valid until the semester label has been affixed. The changes to the student ID are shown in Figure 7.28, which expands Figure 7.27 to include the object flow of the object Student ID. This highlights which actions need and process the object Student ID.

The most important elements of the activity diagram are summarized in Tables 7.1 and 7.2.

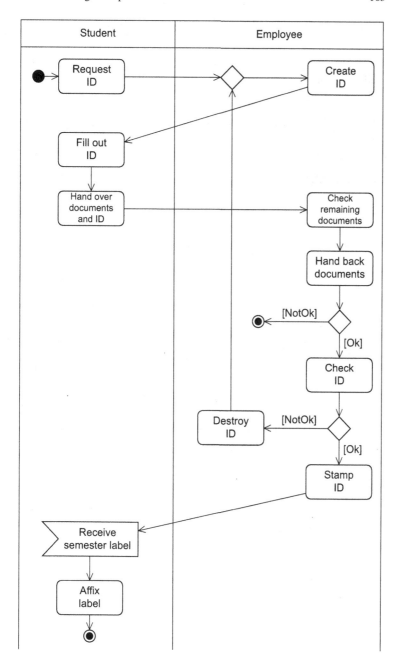

Figure 7.27
Activity diagram "Issue
student ID"

Figure 7.28
Activity diagram "Issue
student ID" with control
and object flow

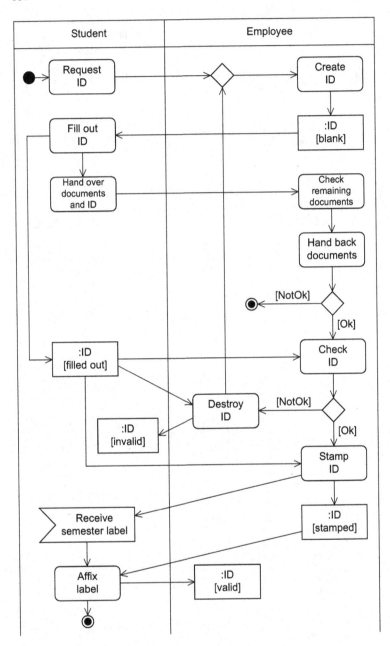

Name	Notation	Description
Action node	Action	Actions are atomic, i.e., they cannot be broken down further
Activity node	Activity	Activities can be broken down further
Initial node	●	Start of the execution of an activity
Activity final node	◉	End of ALL execution paths of an activity
Flow final node	⊗	End of ONE execution path of an activity
Decision node	◇	Splitting of one execution path into two or more alternative execution paths
Merge node	◇	Merging of two or more alternative execution paths into one execution path
Parallelization node	▍	Splitting of one execution path into two or more concurrent execution paths
Synchronization node	▍	Merging of two or more concurrent execution paths into one execution path
Edge	A → B	Connection between the nodes of an activity
Call behavior action	A	Action A refers to an activity of the same name
Object node	Object	Contains data and objects that are created, changed, and read
Parameters for activities	Activity	Contain data and objects as input and output parameters
Parameters for actions (pins)	Action	Contain data and objects as input and output parameters

Table 7.1
Notation elements for the activity diagram

Table 7.2
Notation elements for the
activity diagram, part 2

Name	Notation	Description
Partition		Grouping of nodes and edges within an activity
Send signal action		Transmission of a signal to a receiver
Asynchronous accept (time) event action		Wait for an event E or a time event T
Exception handler		Exception handler is executed instead of the action in the event of an error e
Interruptible activity region		Flow continues on a different path if event E is detected

Chapter 8
All Together Now

In the preceding chapters, we have looked in detail at five UML diagrams that enable us to describe different aspects of a system. In the
examples given, we have seen that the diagrams each realize different
views of a system. Therefore, the diagrams must be interpreted together
as a whole, taking into account how they interact with one another,
rather than each one being considered in isolation. They supplement
each other by illustrating the system to be developed from different perspectives. In this chapter, we model three concrete examples from different application areas that show the interaction between the different
diagrams.

8.1 Example 1: Coffee Machine

An important device encountered time and again in a university is the
coffee machine. Let us look at a filter coffee machine as shown in Figure 8.1. The coffee machine consists of a water tank, a heating plate,
a coffee pot, and a water pipe that leads from the water container to
the filter. When there is water in the tank and the coffee machine is
switched on, the water is heated. The pressure pushes the water up-
wards through the pipe into the filter which contains the ground coffee.
Finally, the brewed coffee flows out of the filter into the coffee pot.
The coffee machine is available in two different versions, one with a
"keep warm" function (model A) and one without (model B). If the water tank is empty and the coffee machine is switched on, in model A
the "keep warm" function is activated. In the same situation, model B
simply switches off.

The use case diagrams in Figure 8.2 describe the functionality of- *Use case diagram*

© Springer International Publishing Switzerland 2015
M. Seidl et al., *UML @ Classroom*, Undergraduate Topics
in Computer Science, DOI 10.1007/978-3-319-12742-2_8

Figure 8.1
Coffee machine

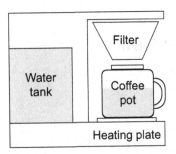

fered by model A and model B. While model A offers the two functions Heat Coffee and Make Coffee, model B can only be used to make coffee. In both cases, we assume very simple coffee machines that are limited to the "core competencies" of coffee machines.

Figure 8.2
Use case diagrams for a coffee machine

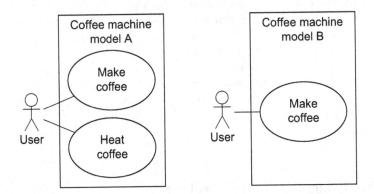

Naturally, users can switch the coffee machine on and off. Maintenance activities such as filling the machine up with coffee or cleaning the filter must also be possible. We have intentionally not modeled these as separate use cases as they are preparatory tasks required to achieve the actual objective—the brewed or warmed up coffee.

Figure 8.3
State machine diagram for coffee machine model B

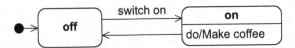

From the description, we can see that both coffee machine models can take the states on and off. Model B exits the state on when the coffee has been made (see Fig. 8.3); in model A, the event switch off must occur for this state change. In model A, the state on can be refined into the states ready (where the heating function is available) and in use (the coffee is being made). The machine can only switch to the state in use when the water tank of the coffee machine is filled (see Fig. 8.4).

State machine diagram

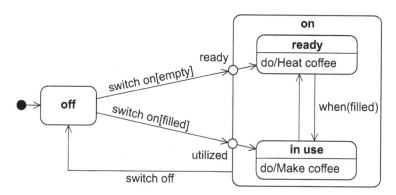

Figure 8.4
State machine diagram for coffee machine model A

The activity diagram in Figure 8.5 describes how to use coffee machine model B. First, the coffee machine is prepared for making the coffee. This involves cleaning the filter, filling the machine with ground coffee, filling the machine with water, and switching the machine on. Note that the filter is always cleaned before the ground coffee is added and that the water is added before the coffee machine is switched on, otherwise the machine switches itself off immediately.

Activity diagram

Apart from these restrictions, the actions can be performed in any order. This is represented in the activity diagram by two concurrent subpaths, each with a separate initial node. The coffee is not made—that is, the water is not poured through the filter—until the two incoming edges of the synchronization node both obtain a token. Our diagram does not cover a situation in which the coffee machine is used without cleaning the filter and without adding ground coffee.

The activity diagram in Figure 8.6 describes the use of model A. As soon as the coffee machine is switched on, it executes the action Heat coffee. When the coffee machine has been fully prepared for making coffee, that is, when ground coffee and water have been added, the keep warm function is switched off and coffee is made. We model this with a synchronization node. The signal Switch off ends the entire process.

Figure 8.5
Activity diagram for coffee
machine model B

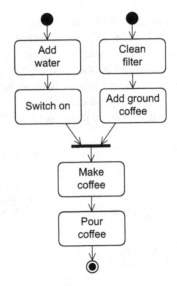

Figure 8.6
Activity diagram for coffee
machine model A

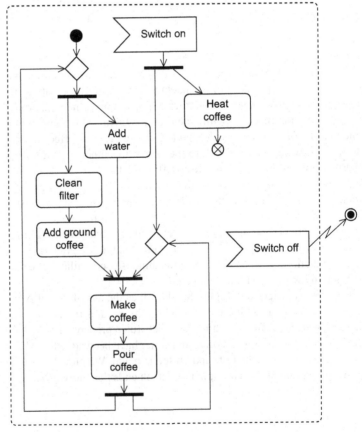

8.2 Example 2: Submission System

UML diagrams are generally used to describe software systems, such
as the student administration system of a university, at which we have
looked in this book from various aspects. Creating a continuous, detailed model of the entire system which could actually be implemented
in executable code would go beyond the scope of this book. However,
we will again extract a part of the system to illustrate the interaction of
the different diagrams. To this end, we will look at a submission system
that is to be used to manage submissions, that is, the students' papers
for assignment tasks. The requirements for this system are as follows:

- Every course in the system has lecturers assigned to it. This is done
  by one of the course administrators, who is also a lecturer. As part of
  a course, lecturers may create tasks and assess papers submitted by
  students. Therefore, the lecturers award points and give feedback.
- The course administrator defines which lecturer assesses which papers. At the end of the course, the course administrator also arranges
  for certificates to be issued. A student's grade is calculated based on
  the total number of points achieved for the submissions handed in.
- Students can take courses and upload papers.
- All users—students and lecturers—can manage their user data, view
  the courses and the tasks set for the courses (provided the respective
  user is involved in the course), and view submitted papers as well as
  grade points. However, students can only view their own papers and
  the related grades. Lecturers can only view the papers assigned to
  them and the grades they have given. The course administrator has
  access rights for all data.
- A course is created and deleted by an administrator.
- When a course is created, at least one administrator must be assigned
  to it. Further course administrators can be assigned at a later point in
  time or assignments to courses can be deleted. The administrator can
  also delete whole courses.
- Information about users and administrators is automatically transferred from another system. Therefore, functions that allow the creation of user data are not necessary.
- All of the system functions can only be used by persons who are
  logged in.

The actors and use cases for the specification above are summarized
in the use case diagram in Figure 8.7. With regard to the actors, we
differentiate between the administrators and all other users, who are in
turn subdivided into lecturers and students. With regard to the lecturers,
we further differentiate course administrators.

Figure 8.7
Use case diagram for a
submission system

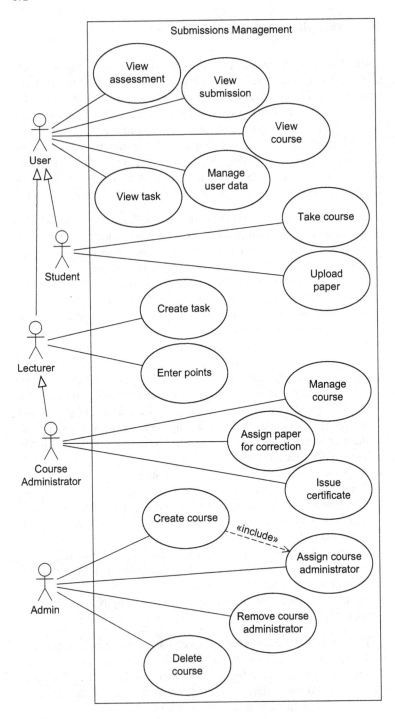

We can derive the use cases directly from the specification above. The use cases are generally not detailed enough for the actual implementation of the system. We now have to highlight exactly which requirements the system must satisfy. However, we do not include this information in the use case diagram as it would make the diagram overloaded and difficult to read. Instead, we document it in the descriptions of the use cases which we learned about in Chapter 3.

The log-in and log-out processes are not represented in the use case diagram as they are not functions desired by the actors but instead contribute to the secure use of the system. Logging in can be considered as a precondition for using the system.

Now that the requirements for the system have been specified, we can zoom into the system and model its structure and behavior. We represent the internal structure of the submission system with the class diagram shown in Figure 8.8. You will notice that all of the actors that appear in the use case diagram are also modeled in the class diagram, even though we stated that they are not part of the system. It is important to understand that in the class diagram, it is the data of the actors that is represented and not the actors themselves. This data is necessary to implement authorizations, the assignment of submissions to students, etc. Information about the users is stored in the class User. We use the attribute authorization to differentiate between administrators (value admin) and all other users (value standard). Administrators can be direct instances of the class User and lecturers and students are modeled by further classes that have an inheritance relationship to User. In principle, this means that it is possible for a lecturer or even a student to be an administrator as well. At first glance, this contradicts our use case diagram, in which the actor Admin is in an inheritance relationship to User. However, if we consider that the actors in the use case diagram represent roles, our class diagram is correct. One person can of course take multiple roles. In the use case diagram, we have only excluded, for example, that an administrator can automatically view information from the courses. If we really wanted to model a strict differentiation here, we would have to introduce a separate class Admin or formulate a constraint that forbids the attribute authorization from taking the value admin for lecturers or students.

In our class diagram, a lecturer becomes a course administrator by being in a gives relationship to a course. Tasks are always assigned to a course, in the same way that submissions are assigned to a task. We model a student's participation in a course using an association class that contains information about the student's total number of points and the grade. Both values are calculated automatically and the attributes are therefore labeled as derived attributes.

Figure 8.8
Class diagram for a sub-
mission system

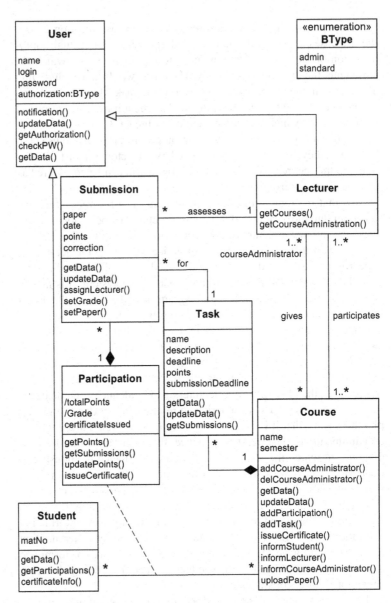

The class diagram in Figure 8.8 does not ensure that a lecturer can only assess tasks of a course in which this lecturer is involved. We have to specify these and other restrictions that are important for the consistency of the overall system. Therefore, additional constraints are required. These can be specified in languages such as the Object Constraint Language (OCL) [36] which is beyond the scope of this book. Then the check that determines whether the instances of a model comply with the specified restrictions can often be perfomed automatically.

In its current form, the class diagram does not contain any platform-specific information, which means that we have not defined what the implementation should look like. For the general specification of the system to be developed, we want to remain at this abstract level in the subsequent steps.

In the next step, we want to model a typical usage scenario of the submission system, that is, how the actors, the system, and the functions that we have specified in the use case diagram interact in a specific situation. We could create an activity diagram to do this. However, as we want to focus on the communication aspect, we use a sequence diagram instead. Figure 8.9 shows the following usage scenario: A student uploads the solved assignment paper to the submission system. The system informs the course administrator that a new assignment paper has been submitted and confirms to the student that the paper has been successfully received. In the sequence diagram, we do not show the action necessary for saving the paper submitted as it is not relevant for the representation of this specific communication process. Via the submission system, the course administrator assigns a lecturer to the paper. Once the system has informed the lecturer that a paper has been assigned, the lecturer assesses the paper. To do this, the lecturer downloads the paper from the submission system and enters the grade in the system. Then the student is informed that the uploaded paper has been graded. The described communication flow takes place not just once but for every task that has to be completed for a course. Therefore, in the sequence diagram in Figure 8.9, the messages described above are enclosed by a loop fragment.

Once all of the tasks have been processed, the course administrator can arrange for the certificates to be issued. The submission system also informs the student of the final grade.

The sequence diagram described in Figure 8.9 reflects the use of the submission system at a very high abstraction level. Although this highlights the general function of the system, many details are still not specified. Therefore, we have to zoom into the system further. To illustrate this, let us look at the activity Issue certificate shown in Figure 8.10. Here we have decided to use an activity diagram to illustrate the detailed process.

Figure 8.9
Communication flows

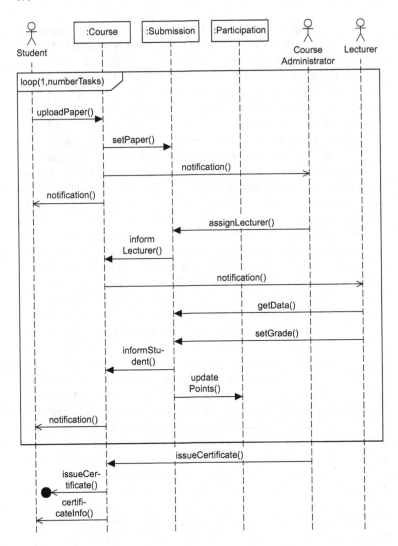

We assume that on the user interface, the course administrator sees an overview of the assigned courses. Firstly, the course administrator selects the course to issue certificates for. The students who have taken the course are displayed. The course administrator can then select whether to issue certificates for all or only for certain students. In the latter case, the administrator must also specify the students who shall obtain certificates. The grades are calculated, sent to the student office, and each student is informed of the grade. Note that for the practical implementation, it is extremely important to model all possible flows in as much

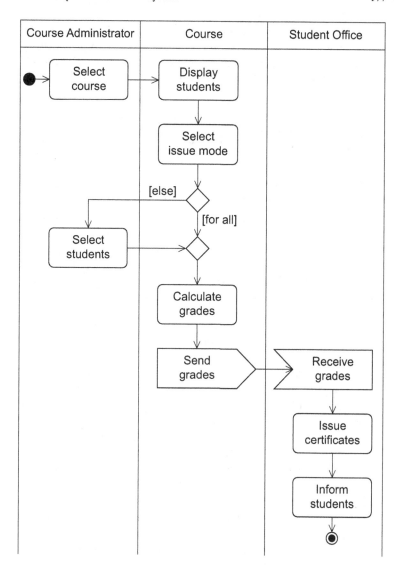

Figure 8.10
Activity diagram for "Issue certificate"

detail as possible and as close to reality as possible. In our activity diagram we have not considered the error situations. It is also not possible in our diagram to manually correct a certificate that has already been issued. All of these cases would also have to be considered. Modeling the processes incorrectly can lead to the system not being accepted by its users. As a result, the increased efficiency expected with the introduction of the system will not be achieved.

To describe the system precisely, it is important also to show the states that the individual components of the system and the system itself can take. As an example, let us look at the state machine diagrams for the submission of a paper (see Fig. 8.11) and for the participation in a course (see Fig. 8.12).

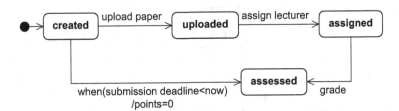

In our system, an instance of class Submission refers to the upload of a paper by a student that then can be assessed by the lecturer. The submission therefore concerns the administration of the file that the student hands over to the lecturer for the assessment, rather than the file itself. When a task is created and released for the students, every student can submit a paper in the system. The submission initially has the state created. It exits this state when the student uploads a paper or when the submission deadline expires—in the latter case the task is assessed with zero points for the student. The submission then changes to the state assessed. If the student submits the solved paper in the system, the submission changes to the state uploaded. It exits this state when the submission is assigned to a lecturer for assessment. Once the assessment has taken place, the submission takes the final state assessed. As the information about a submission is stored for documentation purposes, the submission remains in the state assessed "forever" and no final state is modeled.

The states that a specific participant of a specific course can take are described in a similar way (see Fig. 8.12). In our example, the participation refers to the course participation of a certain student in a certain course. It is documented whether a student has completed a course and, if this is the case, the grade that the student received for this course is saved. When a student has registered for a course, the state of the student's participation in this specific course is initially not assessed. This clearly shows why we describe the states of course participation and not the states of a student. If a student had the state not assessed, it would not be possible to differentiate between different courses that the student has taken. However, what we want to show is the state of a student with reference to a specific course. In the class diagram, this information is taken into account with the association class Participation (see Fig. 8.8).

For a specific course, a student is initially in the state not assessed, then
in the state partially assessed, and finally in the state certificate issued,
unless the student is not assessed at all. This can happen, for example,
if the student was registered but has never actually attended the course
and never completed any activities. The state certificate issued has two
substates—positive and negative. Guards specify which of these states
occurs. These substates can change if a certificate is corrected.

The diagrams in Figures 8.7 to 8.12 illustrate how the different aspects of a submission system and the interaction between these aspects
can be modeled. However, they do not specify any technical details for
the implementation, representing instead a sketch that describes how
the system should look. Once all of the requirements have been documented in the model, the actual implementation can begin. Different
approaches are feasible. One option would be to start the implementation in executable code immediately. However, as no interfaces are
specified, sooner or later the different components will not fit together
anymore, which makes the maintenance of the system more complicated than with carefully designed interfaces.

Therefore, we recommend refining the model further until you have
an exact specification of the system to be developed.

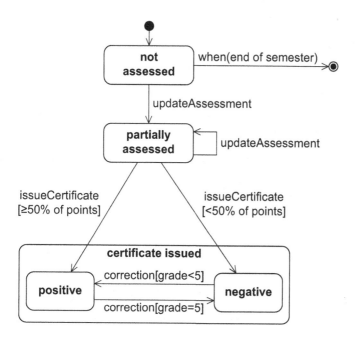

Figure 8.12
State machine diagram for
participation of a student in
a course

8.3 Example 3: Data Type Stack

The final example in this chapter is the modeling of the data structure *Stack*. Elements can be placed on the stack using the push function and removed from the stack using the pop function. The order in which elements are removed follows the LIFO principle (Last In, First Out), which means that pop always delivers the element that was last placed on the stack with push and removes it from the stack. Further functions that the class Stack should support are the determination of the actual size of the stack, that is, the number of elements on the stack, and the query about whether an element is on the stack at all. As we want to realize a stack with no size restriction, we realize it using a recursive data structure as shown in the class diagram in Figure 8.13. The class Stack only knows the uppermost element on the stack. Each element in the stack refers to its direct predecessor. The actual content of a stack element is saved via the private variable content.

Figure 8.13
Class diagram for a stack

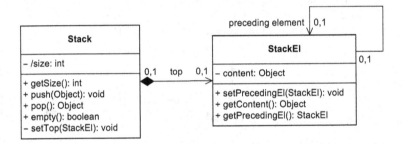

The states that a stack can take are shown in Figure 8.14. Initially the stack is in the state empty. If an element is placed on the stack, the stack changes to the state not empty. Every time push is called, the size of the stack increases by one. Every time pop is called, the size reduces by one. If there is only one element on the stack and pop is called, then the stack changes to the state empty.

Figure 8.14
State machine diagram for
a stack

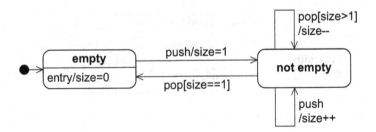

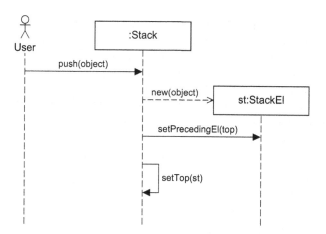

Figure 8.15
Sequence diagram for the
addition of an element to
the stack

The realization of push and pop is shown in the sequence diagrams
8.15 and 8.16. These diagrams are very close to implementations and
reflect how the variables are set.

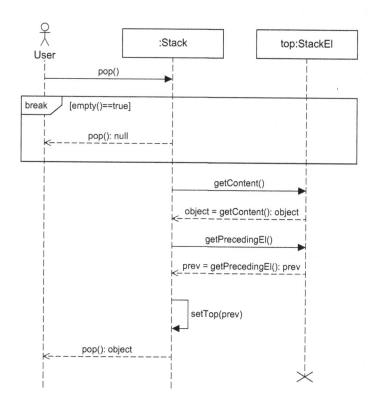

Figure 8.16
Sequence diagram for the
removal of an element
from the stack

To place an object object on the stack, a new instance of StackEl must be created where the attribute content is set to object. The current top element of the stack becomes the predecessor of the new stack, which now becomes the top element on the stack.

The pop operation reverses the effect of a push operation. The content of the current top element is returned and its predecessor becomes the new uppermost element. If there is no element on the stack, the value null is returned.

8.4 Summary

In the three examples discussed in this chapter, we have not only repeated the most important concepts of UML but have also shown how the different diagrams interact. This interaction allows us to describe a system completely without a developer being supplied with all information at once and being overwhelmed by this flood of information. It enables us to focus on specific questions. The information that is shown in the different diagrams redundantly contributes to making the model more consistent overall, as it allows errors to be found at an earlier development stage and more easily.

Chapter 9
Further Topics

In the preceding chapters, we have learned about the basic concepts of object-oriented modeling using numerous language elements of UML. We have learned how to apply these concepts to create UML diagrams. The diagrams offer different views of a complex system, providing abstraction mechanisms to make the complexity of the system manageable. With these mechanisms, UML offers a strong basis for many applications and we could fill many pages by looking at further topics. To give one example, the Systems Modeling Language (SysML) [37] was developed based on UML and extends a subset of UML with special concepts required for modeling complex physical systems.

However, introducing all further topics considering UML would go beyond the objectives of this book. As an outlook, we will briefly consider four further areas here: (i) structuring models, (ii) defining the language of UML, (iii) extension mechanisms in UML, and (iv) model-based software development. Without going into details, these convey a taster of just what is possible with modeling.

9.1 Structuring Models

If a diagram exceeds a certain size, there is a danger that it will become over-complicated. The multitude of model elements, regardless of whether they are classes, actions, states, and so on, very quickly overwhelms a human reader of a diagram. If the overall system consists of multiple subsystems whose elements are only minimally related to one another, then it is desirable to have a mechanism that groups the elements appropriately. For example, in most cases, it is confusing if the user interface elements are mixed with the elements for the database

© Springer International Publishing Switzerland 2015
M. Seidl et al., *UML @ Classroom*, Undergraduate Topics
in Computer Science, DOI 10.1007/978-3-319-12742-2_9

access. In literature, different criteria for grouping elements have been identified [23]:

- *Functional cohesion*: elements with similar purpose are grouped.
- *Informational cohesion*: elements that are strongly related to one another but only weakly related to other elements are grouped.
- *Distribution structure*: when developing a distributed system, the elements are grouped according to their physical distribution—for example, elements on the client and elements on the server.
- *Structuring of the development*: the structuring reflects the division of the development tasks. This is particularly important if there is a team of developers involved in developing the system. Clearly defined responsibilities and interfaces avoid situations in which team members get in each other's way.

Package diagram

In programming languages, the concept of the "namespace" was introduced to enable structuring. In Java for example, this is realized in the form of *packages*. UML offers the *package diagram* for this purpose.

9.1.1 Packages

Package

A *package* allows you to group model elements, such as classes, data types, activities, and states, etc., but can also contain packages itself. The notation for a package is a rectangle with a smaller rectangle on top in the left corner—similar to an index card. The large rectangle contains the elements that the package groups (see Fig. 9.1(a)). The small rectangle contains the package name. If the package content is not relevant, the package name can also be positioned in the large rectangle (see Fig. 9.1(b)). Alternatively, the package content can be represented outside the large rectangle and connected to the package by lines that end in a circle containing a cross on the side of the package (see Fig. 9.1(c)).

Namespace

A model element may be included in a maximum of one package directly. This inclusion in a package defines the namespace in which an element is visible. The name of an element must be unique within a namespace. However, different elements may have the same name within different namespaces. Thus, if package P1 contains a class C, it cannot be confused with class C in package P2. The package membership is thus a qualifying factor, allowing a clear differentiation between different elements with the same name. The unique name of an element is specified by prepending the package name followed by two colons. This gives us, for example, the two unique names P1::C and P2::C.

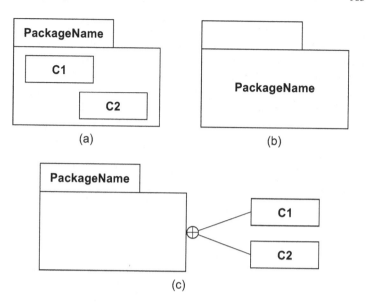

Figure 9.1
Notation alternatives for
package diagrams

9.1.2 Importing Elements/Packages

Elements of a specific package can reference one another and communicate with one another without any further details provided this is not restricted by visibilities and navigation directions. For example, an element E that is located in a package P1 can also be used in a package P2 provided P2 does not contain an element with the same name E and P2 is included directly or indirectly in P1. Elements from other packages can either be imported or referenced using qualified names. All elements of the imported package with the corresponding visibility become visible in the importing package. These elements can thus be referenced directly. The name of an imported element is added to the namespace of the package and can then be used without qualification (that is, without namespace::).

Think back to the class diagram (Chapter 4)—there we defined visibilities of attributes, operations, and roles. In doing so, we also became familiar with the visibility package, notated by ˜ (see Tab. 4.1 on page 59). This visibility means that the attributes, operations, and roles are only visible for elements within the same package.

Import relationships are denoted by a dashed arrow that points away from the importer and is labeled with «import». Of course, only elements that are visible externally can be imported, such as class C1 in package P3, which is imported by package P1 (Fig. 9.2).

Importing packages   A package can import entire packages in this way. For example, in Figure 9.2, package P1 imports package P2. This makes all visible elements of the imported package visible in the namespace of the importing package. This is handled and noted like every other import relationship.

For a more detailed examination of this topic, see [23].

Figure 9.2
Import relationship

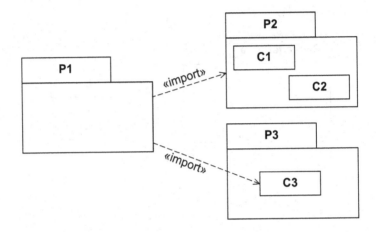

9.2 The UML Metamodel

Metamodel   Critical readers will ask themselves how we know how to apply the concepts of the different diagrams. This is described in the *metamodel*. A metamodel is a model that describes a modeling language. It thus states something *about* other models, a fact which is expressed by the Greek prefix "meta", which means "about". In the same way that elements of a model are referred to as model elements, the elements of a metamodel are referred to as metamodel elements.

Superstructure   The UML metamodel, the *superstructure* [35], specifies UML in the form of class diagrams. We use class diagrams to describe which elements a UML diagram may contain and how these elements are applied. However, this also means that a class diagram, which is part of UML, is itself specified by a class diagram. This is comparable with programming languages. Here it is possible and common to write a compiler for C in C, for example. With the concepts that we know from the class diagram, we can now specify modeling languages ourselves. The classes no longer represent persons, courses, and so on but rather language concepts, such as classes, associations, and generalizations, etc. Figure 9.3 shows an example of a simple modeling language that is very similar to the UML class diagram and is itself represented in the form of a class diagram. This metamodel is similar to the metamodel of the real UML class diagram but it is heavily simplified. Almost all classes inherit from the class NamedElement. All direct and indirect instances of this class have a name that identifies them uniquely. Associations are described by a separate class. In contrast, a generalization is represented only as a relationship between classes. Of course, we could also model the generalization as a separate class. This would allow us to specify further properties for the generalization, as in "real" UML. For example, in UML, a generalization can be described as disjoint or overlapping (see 4.6.2), which is something we cannot do in our simplified metamodel.

The syntax of UML introduced here is also referred to as *abstract syntax*. If we were to draw an instance of the metamodel from Figure 9.3—that is, an object model—an association would be depicted as a separate element that connects other elements. An abstract class is then identified by the isAbstract flag. This notation is not particularly user-friendly. We have expressed associations simply with a direct connection between the classes that are in a relationship with one another and we have specifically identified abstract classes. This type of notation is more intuitive for human users. Therefore, in addition to the abstract syntax, UML defines the *concrete syntax*, which is a notation optimized for humans.

Abstract syntax

Concrete syntax

Of course, there are many other important details about metamodels and metamodeling that we could discuss. For example, the obvious question is how the language used to create the metamodel is defined. For this purpose UML has the *infrastructure* [34] which introduces the required concepts. This is the metametamodel of UML. We could continue these definitions to infinity but the specification does not go beyond the metametalevel.

Infrastructure

9.3 UML Extension Mechanisms

As a general purpose modeling language, UML provides a stable basis for a wide variety of requirements. It is not defined for specific application domains or for any specific technology. However, in some circumstances, UML is too general and using it involves a considerable amount of effort. In such cases, the use of a language optimized for the given domain and therefore offering special concepts is advantageous.

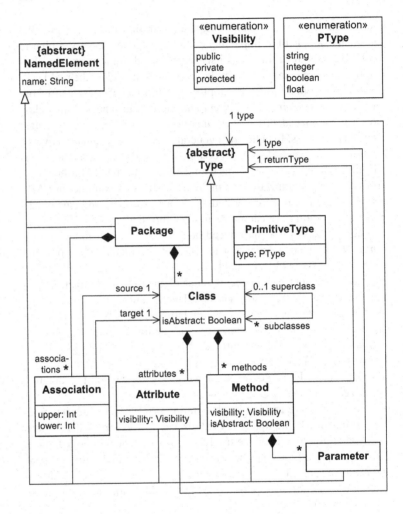

Figure 9.3
Heavily simplified meta-
model of a class diagram

This type of language can be defined in one of the following three ways:

- Creation of a new metamodel
- Extension and modification of the UML metamodel
- Extension of the UML metamodel with language-inherent mecha-
  nisms

Creation of a new
metamodel

If the description of the systems to be modeled requires language
concepts that are very different to the language concepts of UML, it is
probably more practical not to use the language definition of UML and
to define your own modeling language by creating a *new metamodel*.

As an alternative to creating a new metamodel, you can also *extend and modify* the UML metamodel in accordance with your requirements. In this case, you introduce new metaclasses and new associations between the metaclasses or overwrite existing properties. This type of extension is also referred to as a heavyweight extension. In many cases, it makes the interoperability of modeling tools more difficult, as of course not all of the tools support the extended metamodel.

Extension and modification of the UML metamodel

UML itself offers *language-inherent extension mechanisms*, that is, extension options that are provided in the language itself. These are already defined at the metametamodel level, that is, in the UML infrastructure. The extensions are thus implemented in a controlled way; existing language concepts can only be extended and made more specific and they must not be changed or generalized. This lightweight extension mechanism retains the interoperability between the different modeling tools. These lightweight extensions are based on *stereotypes* and *profiles*, which we will look at more closely below.

Extension of the UML metamodel with language-inherent mechanisms

9.3.1 Stereotypes and Profiles

In Section 9.2, we saw that the UML metamodel itself is also a model. It describes the language elements of UML. The metamodel defines, for example, that a class diagram contains classes, associations, and generalizations, etc. The classes of the metamodel are referred to as metaclasses. A *stereotype* is a special metaclass in the UML metamodel. It allows you to extend any metaclass with additional meta-attributes (tag definitions) and to make it more specific using additional constraints. A metaclass for which a stereotype has been defined remains unchanged. In the simplest case, stereotypes are used to classify metaclasses without introducing additional meta-attributes and constraints.

Stereotype

A stereotype is denoted like a class, with the keyword «stereotype» above the name in the first compartment. The second compartment usually contains the meta-attributes. The constraints can be specified either after the meta-attributes or as a note. You can also specify a pictogram for a stereotype. This symbol is used later with the corresponding elements. Figure 9.4 shows an example of a stereotype. The stereotype Entity contains two meta-attributes, author and year, as well as two constraints. One constraint states that the values of the meta-attribute author can have a maximum of ten characters, with the other constraint stating that the value of the meta-attribute year must be smaller than 2006.

A stereotype extends one or more metaclasses. This *extension relationship* is depicted as an arrow with a continuous line and filled arrowhead. The arrow points away from the stereotype to the metaclass. The

Extension relationship

Figure 9.4
Specification of the stereotype "Entity"

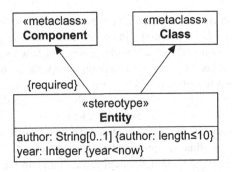

extended metaclass is identified with the keyword «metaclass». Stereotypes defined in this way are optional, meaning that you do not have
to use them in the modeling. You can also use model elements that are
based on the original definition of the metaclass. To force the use of a
stereotype, the extension relationship must be identified as mandatory
through the use of the keyword {required}. In Figure 9.4, the stereotype
Entity is thus optional for the metaclass Class but mandatory for the
metaclass Component.

Stereotypes can be connected to one another via an inheritance relationship. In this context, they can be defined as abstract. A derived
stereotype inherits all meta-attributes, constraints, and extension relationships of its higher level stereotypes. Figure 9.5 shows an example
of inheritance for stereotypes. The stereotypes Entity and Session are
derived from the abstract stereotype Bean. The keyword {abstract} in
the name field identifies Bean as abstract. The stereotype Session introduces a new meta-attribute state. The extension relationship between
Component and Bean is mandatory, meaning that when a component is
modeled, the stereotype Bean must always be used with a specific value.

Profile   *Profiles* group stereotypes defined for a specific purpose. A profile
is a special form of the package that we learned about at the beginning
of this chapter. Therefore, a profile has the same notation as a package,

Figure 9.5
Example of inheritance
with stereotypes [35]

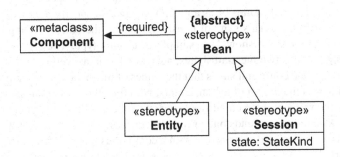

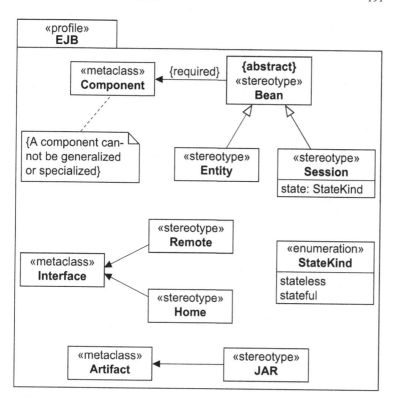

Figure 9.6
Example of a profile [35]

with the keyword «profile» prepended to the profile name. Figure 9.6 shows an example of a profile [35] for Enterprise JavaBeans (EJB).

9.3.2 Applying Stereotypes of a Profile

To use stereotypes in a specific application, you must first integrate the profile that contains the stereotypes. You do this with a dashed arrow with an open arrowhead pointing away from the package of the application towards the profile. This arrow is labeled with the keyword «apply». This imports the stereotypes defined in the profile into the namespace of the package. Figure 9.7 shows an example of the application of a stereotype. The package with the name UserModel contains a component Customer with the stereotype Session. The value for the meta-attribute state is specified in a note. The symbol that appears in the upper right corner of Customer designates components in UML notation.

Figure 9.7
Example of the application
of a stereotype

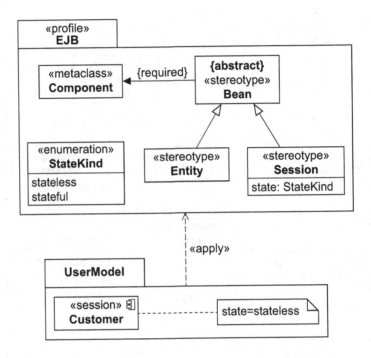

9.4 Model-Based Software Development

Models often serve as construction plans for software. For the developers, they stipulate which properties the end product should have. They
specify the requirements that a software system must fulfill and describe
which components occur in the system and how these components interact. Models are thus the basis for the development of executable code,
which is traditionally created by human programmers. If the model and
the code are to be kept up-to-date, any changes made must be implemented in both the model and the code. This involves additional effort.

The next step in simplifying the software development process is
obvious—namely the automatic generation of the code from the models.
This brings us to model-based software development. Models are significantly more than pretty pictures for documenting a software system
and for use as sketches or blueprints. In model-based software development, the executable system is created from the models. Here, therefore,
models have the same value as code.

Model-based software
development

In *model-based software development (MBSD)*, source code is created partially or completely from models. Programming is thus replaced
by modeling. The models must describe the function of the system to
be developed as precisely as possible. The semantics of the modeling

languages used must be defined unambiguously so that the language elements can be transformed into code uniquely. General purpose modeling languages such as UML may be very flexible but they are often too general for specific applications, meaning that specific concepts are missing. For example, in the description of a web application, the "hyperlink" is a central concept that is not available in UML. Therefore, in model-based software development, smaller languages tailored to the respective domain are often used. These languages are also referred to as *domain-specific languages (DSL)*. Of course, they can be defined based on UML, as we saw in the previous section on stereotypes and profiles.

General purpose modeling language

Domain-specific language (DSL)

In MBSD, models are transformed into other models that, for example, contain specific details about the target platform of the system. Alternatively, executable code is generated in common programming languages. The expert knowledge that is required to create an executable program is therefore invested in these model transformations. It is thus retained in an infrastructure that can be reused again. In recent years, numerous special languages and frameworks have been introduced for creating these transformations.

The aim of MBSD is to significantly simplify the development of applications by replacing programming with modeling, without the developers or modelers having to have specific knowledge about the platforms used.

To summarize, model-based software development aims to provide the following advantages [49]:

- *Increase the speed of development:* code, which is often repeated, is created automatically and adapted to the current situation. There is a significant decrease in "copy and paste" activities.
- *Increase the quality of the software:* the automatic transformations reduce the risk of errors in the implementation. The code is also created independently of the abilities and experience of a developer. Thanks to the tool support, the implementation of the software architecture is better.
- *Central troubleshooting:* errors only have to be corrected in the model and they are then eliminated in the corresponding code parts when the transformation is executed again. The transformation rules may have to be adapted if they no longer match the requirements. However, this only has to be done once.
- *Increase the reuse:* modeling languages, in particular DSLs, only have to be created once. They aggregate expert knowledge that can then be used in different projects.

- *Handling complexity through abstraction:* the complexity of the implementation language remains hidden in the modeling languages; technical implementation details do not have to be considered.
- *Portability:* the code can be generated for different platforms from one model.

Models are used not only to generate the implementation of the system to be developed; they are also used for simulations, for analyzing system properties, for generating test cases, and for verifying and validating the system to be developed. Model-based software development can be implemented in different ways. For a detailed introduction to this topic, see [6, 49].

References

1. J. Bézivin and P.A. Muller. UML: The Birth and Rise of a Standard Modeling Notation. In *The Unified Modeling Language. UML'98: Beyond the Notation*, volume 1618 of *Lecture Notes in Computer Science*, pages 1–8. Springer, 1999.
2. G.M. Birtwhistle, O.J. Dahl, B. Myhrhaug, and K. Nygaard. *Simula Begin*. Chartwell-Bratt Ltd., 1979.
3. K. Bittner and I. Spence. *Use Case Modeling*. Addison-Wesley, 2002.
4. J. Bloch. *Effective Java: A Programming Language Guide*. Addison-Wesley Professional, 2. edition, 2014.
5. G. Booch. Object-Oriented Development. *IEEE Transactions on Software Engineering*, 12(2):211–221, 1986.
6. M. Brambilla, J. Cabot, and M. Wimmer. *Model-Driven Software Engineering in Practice*. Morgan & Claypool, 2012.
7. M. Brandsteidl, T. Mayerhofer, M. Seidl, and C. Huemer. Replacing traditional classroom lectures with lecture videos: an experience report. In *Educators' Symposium @ MODELS 2012*, pages 21–27. ACM, 2012.
8. M. Brandsteidl, M. Seidl, and G. Kappel. Teaching Models @ BIG: On Efficiently Assessing Modeling Concepts. In *Educators' Symposium @ MODELS 2009*, 2009.
9. M. Brandsteidl, M. Seidl, M. Wimmer, C. Huemer, and G. Kappel. Teaching Models @ BIG — How to Give 1000 Students an Understanding of the UML. In *Promoting Software Modeling Through Active Education, Educators' Symposium @ MODELS 2008*, pages 64–68. Warsaw University of Technology, 2008.
10. M. Brandsteidl, K. Wieland, and C. Huemer. New Media in Teaching UML in the Large - an Experience Report. *ECEASST*, 34, 2010.
11. M. Brandsteidl, K. Wieland, and C. Huemer. Novel Communication Channels in Software Modeling Education. In *MoDELS Workshops*, volume 6627 of *Lecture Notes in Computer Science*, pages 40–54. Springer, 2010.
12. L.F. Capretz. A Brief History of the Object-Oriented Approach. *ACM SIGSOFT Software Engineering Notes*, 28(2):1–10, 2003.
13. L. Cardelli and P. Wegner. On Understanding Types, Data Abstraction, and Polymorphism. *ACM Computing Surveys*, 17(4):471–522, 1985.
14. P.P.S. Chen. The Entity-Relationship Model — Toward a Unified View of Data. *ACM Transactions on Database Systems*, 1(1):9–36, 1976.
15. A. Cockburn. Goals and Use Cases. *Journal of Object-Oriented Programming*, 10(5):35–40, 1997.

© Springer International Publishing Switzerland 2015
M. Seidl et al., *UML @ Classroom*, Undergraduate Topics
in Computer Science, DOI 10.1007/978-3-319-12742-2

16. A. Cockburn. *Writing Effective Use Cases*. Addison-Wesley Longman, 2001.

17. S. Finger and J.R. Dixon. A review of research in mechanical engineering design. Part I: Descriptive, prescriptive, and computer-based models of design processes. *Research in engineering design*, 1(1):51–67, 1989.

18. M. Fowler. *Patterns of Enterprise Application Architecture*. Addison-Wesley Longman, 2003.

19. M. Fowler. *UML Distilled: A Brief Guide to the Standard Object Modeling Language*. Addison-Wesley, revised edition, 2003.

20. E. Gamma, R. Helm, R. Johnson, and J. Vlissides. *Design Patterns. Elements of Reusable Object-Oriented Software*. Prentice Hall, 1. edition, 1994.

21. C. Ghezzi and M. Jazayeri. *Programming Language Concepts*. Wiley, 3. edition, 1997.

22. D. Harel. Statecharts: A Visual Formalism for Complex Systems. *Science of Computer Programming*, 8(3):231–274, 1987.

23. M. Hitz, G. Kappel, E. Kapsammer, and W. Retschitzegger. *UML@Work. Objektorientierte Modellierung mit UML 2 (in German)*. dpunkt.verlag, 3. edition, 2005.

24. J.R. Holmevik. Compiling SIMULA: A Historical Study of Technological Genesis. *IEEE Annals of the History of Computing*, 16(4):25–37, 1994.

25. J.D. Ichbiah, J.G.P. Barnes, R.J. Firth, and M. Woodger. *Rationale for the Design of the Ada Programming Language*. Cambridge University Press, 1986.

26. D. Jackson. Software Abstractions. *The MIT Press*, 2011.

27. I. Jacobson, M. Christerson, P. Jonsson, and G. Overgaard. *Object-Oriented Software Engineering, A Use Case Driven Approach*. Addison-Wesley Longman, 1992.

28. A.C. Kay. The Early History of Smalltalk. *ACM SIGPLAN Notices*, 28(3):69–95, 1993.

29. J. Kramer. Is abstraction the key to computing? *Communications of the ACM*, 50(4):36–42, 2007.

30. L. Maciaszek. *Requirements Analysis and System Design*. Pearson Education, 3. edition, 2007.

31. B. Meyer. *Touch of Class, Learning to Program Well with Objects and Contracts*. Springer, 2. edition, 2013.

32. H. Mössenböck. *C# to the Point*. Pearson Addison Wesley, 2004.

33. Object Management Group. OMG Homepage. http://www.omg.org.

34. Object Management Group. OMG Unified Modeling Language (UML), Infrastructure. Technical Report Version 2.4.1, OMG, August 2011.

35. Object Management Group. OMG Unified Modeling Language (UML), Superstructure. Technical Report Version 2.4.1, OMG, August 2011.

36. Object Management Group. Object Constraint Language. Technical Report Version 2.3.1, OMG, May 2012.

37. Object Management Group. OMG Systems Modeling Language (SysML). Technical report, OMG, 2012.

38. Object Management Group. XML Metadata Interchange (XMI). Technical Report Version 2.4.2, OMG, April 2014.

39. G. Övergaard and K. Palmkvist. *Use Cases: Patterns and Blueprints*. Addison-Wesley Longman, 2005.

40. K. Pohl. *Requirements Engineering: Fundamentals, Principles, and Techniques*. Springer, 2010.

41. W. Reisig. *Understanding Petri Nets*. Springer, 2013.

42. J. Rumbaugh, M. Blaha, W. Premerlani, F. Eddy, and W. Lorensen. *Object-Oriented Modeling and Design*. Prentice Hall, 1991.

43. J. Rumbaugh, I. Jacobson, and G. Booch. *The Unified Modeling Language Reference Manual*. Pearson Education, 2. edition, 2004.

44. N. Russell, W.M.P. van der Aalst, A.H.M. ter Hofstede, and P. Wohed. On the suitability of UML 2.0 activity diagrams for business process modelling. In *3rd Asia-Pacific Conference on Conceptual Modelling*, pages 95–104. Australian Computer Society, Inc., 2006.

45. G. Schneider and J. Winters. *Applying Use Cases: A Practical Approach*. Addison-Wesley, 2001.

46. M. Scholz, P. Kaufmann, and M. Seidl. Making UML "hip": A First Experience Report on Using Modern Teaching Tools for Object-Oriented Modelling. In *EduSymp @ MODELS 2013*, volume 1134 of *CEUR Workshop Proceedings*. CEUR-WS.org, 2013.

47. B. Selic. The Pragmatics of Model-Driven Development. *IEEE Software*, 20(5):19–25, 2003.

48. H. Stachowiak. *Allgemeine Modelltheorie (in German)*. Springer, 1973.

49. T. Stahl and M. Völter. *Model-Driven Software Development: Technology, Engineering, Management*. Wiley, 2006.

50. B. Stroustrup. *The C++ Programming Language*. Addison Wesley, 4. edition, 2013.

51. I.E. Sutherland. Sketchpad: A Man-Machine Graphical Communication System. *Simulation*, 2(5):R–3–R–20, 1964.

52. Wikipedia. System. `http://en.wikipedia.org/wiki/System`, 2014.

Index

absolute time
  sequence diagram, 130
  state machine diagram, 94
abstract
  abstract actor, **29**, 39
  abstract class, **70**, 72, 78, 81
    notation, 73
  abstract data type, 12
  abstract operation, 73
  abstract syntax, 187
  abstract use case, **32**, 44
abstraction, 3
accept event action, **144–145**, 160, 162
accept time event action, 144
action, 86, **143–146**, 150, 152, 153
  accept event, 144–145
  accept event action, **144**, 160, 162
  call, 145–146
  call behavior, 145–146
  call behavior action, 145
  call operation action, 146
  event-based, 144–145
  exception handling, 159, 160
  execution permission, 146, 147
  input parameter, 155
  output parameter, 155
  partitioning, 156
  send signal action, 145
  time accept event action, 144
active object, 110
activity
  activity diagram, **142**, 143, 144
    call behavior, 145–146
  state machine diagram
    decision node, 90

do, **86**, 87
entry, **86**, 88, 92, 101
exit, **86**, 87, 88, 92
history state, 101
internal, 86
internal transition, 92
pseudostate, 89
syntax, 88
transition, 87, 102
activity diagram, 20, 138, **141–166**, 169, 175
activity final node, **151**, 153
actor
  activity diagram, **157**, 158, 162
  sequence diagram, **109**, 175
  use case diagram, 23, **25–27**, 33, 36, 37, 39, 171, 173
    abstract, **29**, 39
    identification, **34–35**, 42
    inheritance, **28–29**, 34
Ada, 12
after, *see* relative time
aggregation, **67–69**, 78–79
  composition, 68–69
  shared, 68
alt operator, 116
alternative interaction, *see alt* operator
alternative transition, 90
anonymous object, 51
any receive event, 95
assert operator, 126
asserted interaction, *see assert* operator
association
  class diagram, 60–65
    bidirectional, 61

© Springer International Publishing Switzerland 2015
M. Seidl et al., *UML @ Classroom*, Undergraduate Topics
in Computer Science, DOI 10.1007/978-3-319-12742-2